Earth Changes

Teachings by Phylos: Bringing the Divine Into Your Earth Plane Life

Disclaimer

The source of the information in this book is higher consciousness, not scientific or medical research. The information in this book is intended to help you to grow spiritually, not to diagnose or treat disease. Consult your physician or other health care provider for advice about your health and for the diagnoses of any ailments you may have. Consult your physician or other health care provider before you start or stop taking any medication, before you begin or end any specific diet or course of treatment, and before you apply the processes in this book to your life. The author and publisher assume no responsibility whatever for any adverse consequences which may result from the application of the suggestions in this book.

***

Cover painting by Carin Nieuwenhout
Cover design by Julie Burnett
Authors' photograph by Leela Gort
Energy point by Erik Kleinepier

***

Copyright © 2005 by Jeroen Kuyper and Froukje Buma.
All rights reserved. No part of this book may be reproduced by any means or in any form whatsoever without written permission from the author or his wife, except for brief quotations embodied in literary articles or reviews. The authors can be reached at www.ascendedmasters.nl.

ISBN: 1-4196-0301-9

Library of Congress Control Number: 2005924053

To order additional copies, please contact us.
BookSurge, LLC
www.booksurge.com
1-866-308-6235
orders@booksurge.com

JEROEN KUYPER

EARTH CHANGES

Teachings by Phylos: Bringing the Divine Into Your Earth Plane Life

2005

Earth Changes
Teachings by Phylos: Bringing the Divine
Into Your Earth Plane Life

To Sheri M., our sweet and loving friend, who received an extremely severe sentence—nearly seven years in prison—for drug offences. Sheri is a lovely woman who has been drug free for a long time and who is firmly on her spiritual path.

Dear Sheri. Phylos, Froukje, and I send you love and light. May the bizarre circumstances in which you find yourself be resolved quickly. We pray for you and all the other Sheris in similar circumstances.

CONTENTS

Gratitude	ix
Introduction	xiii
Introduction by Phylos	xvii
Part 1: Earth Changes	1
1. Setting the Energy: Opening to the Higher Light	3
2. Visit To Castle Lake: The Lemurians	7
3. The Personality and Its Presence on Earth	13
4. Why Write This Book?	19
5. Meditation: Expanding through the Physical Boundary	25
6. The Nature of Consciousness and Its Layers	29
7. Meditation: Opening to Your Inner Being	37
8. Time and Space	41
9. Beings of Light	49
10. Meditation: Deepening Connections	57
11. The Chosen Ones and Ascension	59
12. Words of Good-bye	69
Part 2: Living Well	73
13. Soul Contact	75
14. Playing the Earth Game: The Rules of the Game	87
15. Doorways	93
16. Meditation: Catching Higher Thoughts	99
17. Higher Love, Creativity, and Intent	101
18. The Power of Thoughts	109
19. Selfishness	121
20. Meditation: Visiting the Higher Realms	129
21. Exercise: Expanding Consciousness	133
22. Building Consciousness	143
23. Meditation: Creating Your Perfect Day	151

24. Meditation: Changing a Habit	155
25. Words of Good-bye	159
Part 3: Divine Intervention	163
26. Why Is There Divine?	165
27. Meditation: Finding Divine Energy	171
28. The Divine Is in Everything	173
29. Meditation: Revitalizing in the Divine Light	179
30. Levels of Growth	183
31. Meditation: Entering the Higher Dimensions of Your Being	195
32. Divine Intervention	199
33. Meditation: Entering Other Dimensions	203
34. Being a Focus of Light for Everyone	207
35. Meditation: Manifesting Light	215
36. World Crises	219
37. Visit to Castle Lake: Indian Lives	223
38. Meditation: Absorbing Light	229
39. Earth Changes	233
40. At Last, We Visit Medicine Lake	243
41. Revitalizing Meditation	247
42. Remembering Your Higher State Throughout the Day	251
43. Rituals and Ancient Knowledge	259
44. Words of Good-bye	267
Biographies	269
Energy Point	271
Contact us	273
Notes	275

GRATITUDE

Froukje and I want to express our deep gratitude to the following persons and masters:

To our beloved editor, Inger Smith, for transforming our Dutch English into readable English while preserving Phylos's energy transmissions. Thank you for your dedication, for your precision, and for the love and light you radiate.

To our dear friend, Kay Watters, for editing the early drafts of the manuscript. Thank you so much for your support, love, and care.

To Brigitte Damen for transcribing all our audiotapes with great perseverance, and for caring so lovingly for our pets while we were at Mount Shasta.

To our cover artist, Carin Nieuwenhout, thank you for the beautiful cover and all the sweet love that you are and that you put into this painting.

To Leela Gort for the cover photograph you made of us. Thank you for the joy and ease with which you do your work.

To Erik Kleinepier for creating the energy point. Thank you for your clear vision and inspiration.

To our dear Mount Shasta friends: Polly Elliot, Mick Laugs, Mary Pat Mahan, and Inger Smith. Thank you for all your love and support, for the wonderful time we shared at Mount Shasta, and for holding a focus for this book.

To Prema Baba Swamiji (Donald Schnell) for reading and endorsing our manuscript, and for the wonderful connection we developed with you as our new spiritual teacher. Meeting you was a profound gift. Being in your presence is indescribably wonderful. We love you and your dear wife, Leelananda, (Marilyn Diamond), from the bottom of our hearts. Your book *The Initiation* is a pearl.

To Julie Barnett for her cover design.

To Freddy Julsing for believing in our project right from the start. Thank you for all your light, advice, and support. We were saddened to hear that you passed into the greater light on January 15, 2005.

To Aurelia Louise Jones, author of *Telos,* for her sweet support and encouragement. Thank you for accepting our book for publication—before your own book became so successful that you stopped publishing for others.

To Willy van Moerkerk for helping Jeroen take his guides seriously from the beginning.

To our first spiritual teacher and dear friend, John Kalse, for his endless acceptance and loving guidance.

To our teachers, Sanaya Roman and Duane Packer, and their guides Orin and DaBen, who created the beautiful *Awakening Your Light Body* course and its sequels. Thank you so much for providing this path, which helped us grow fast, find our higher purpose, and discover our channeling abilities.

To our friends, Craig Wallin and Sherri Bilbro, whom we met at Panther Meadows Campground. Thank you for reading our manuscript and giving us your beautiful feedback. By following your dream, you set a wonderful example for us.

To all the sweet students of our Phylos-Saint Germain group for their receptivity to the energies. Thank you for being our guinea pigs as we developed new materials and brought through meditations from the masters.

To the many students, friends, and others who have read our manuscript for their wonderful feedback.

To the masters, our beloved guides: Phylos, Saint Germain, and Kuthumi for holding us in their light, and for supporting us with their unconditional love and infinite patience.

We feel deep love and gratitude for all of you. Thank you.

INTRODUCTION

In August 1996, my wife, Froukje, and I attended a three-day *Light Body* seminar in Ashland, Oregon.[1] Afterward we took some time to visit nearby Mount Shasta since we had heard that it was a very spiritual place.

While we were walking on the mountain for the first time, I began to hear a voice "talking" in my head. In recent years I had become aware of my sensitivity to these kinds of phenomena. A few years before, while I was attending another course on spiritual growth, I had seen two human-like beings who talked to me while I was in meditation. Later I understood that these beings were guides. Most remarkable about the voice on Mount Shasta was that it spoke to me in English instead of in my own Dutch language.

The voice announced itself as Phylos, one of the ascended masters of Mount Shasta. The year before, I had read a book about the ascended masters so I knew about them and about Phylos, but I had hardly expected to be in contact with them myself. At first I thought that maybe the voice was just my imagination, but it insisted that it was indeed the same Phylos I had read about.

During that first contact, Phylos told us about upcoming earth changes. He also said that the masters had changed their frequencies slightly so that humans could no longer meet them in person or find their Radiant Temple.[2] He would explain the reasons for this later.

He also told me that in order for him to come through I had to walk uphill just as I was doing at that moment. Phylos explained that the masters live in higher dimensions than we do and that Mount Shasta is one of the few places in the world where the earth's energy is intertwined with the energy of their higher dimensions.

By walking upward, I would be able to bridge the gap between the energies of the earth and those of the higher dimensions thereby making it possible for him to transmit high information through me.

It would also be necessary that Froukje be with me. He described her energy as a kind of umbrella, functioning as an antenna that gathers and focuses the energy. With Froukje holding a focus for me, Phylos's energy could come through at a much higher level than if I were there alone. Later we learned that another Ascended master, Saint Germain, was helping Froukje hold the energy.

Phylos invited us to come back to the mountain because he intended to dictate a book called *Earth Changes* through us.

At that time, we could not conceive of coming to the United States and to Mount Shasta that often. However, as I write this introduction we are about to leave for our ninth visit. Somehow money is always there to let us come back again.

We bought recording equipment and went back to Mount Shasta, and Phylos did as promised. Just a few minutes after we began our first walk he began dictating. He announced that the book would be divided into three parts. The first part would give general information about earth changes and the way the universe works. The second part would contain guidelines for living in the denser energies of the earth. The third part would handle the ways in which the Divine intervenes in the earth plane. Guided meditations throughout the book would provide opportunities for readers to experience the teachings of preceding chapters. Thus the book would be both theoretical and experiential.

We feel gifted that this high master has chosen to work with us. Every time we connect with him we feel an enormous amount of love and bliss pouring through us. Unfortunately these wonderful experiences cannot be translated into words. However, Phylos has promised that whoever is reading the book or doing the meditations will receive energy transmissions from the masters and may experience some of the expanded states of consciousness about which he is teaching us.

Jeroen Kuyper, February 2005

INTRODUCTION BY PHYLOS

Mount Shasta, lower slopes

Mount Shasta

Welcome, I am Phylos. I am an ascended master and I speak to you from high up on our beautiful mountain, Mount Shasta. It is my honor and pleasure to bring our messages of love and support down to you in these pages. I say "our messages" because I speak on behalf of other masters as well.

Strong new energies are coming to the earth

We entitled this book Earth Changes because strong new energies are coming to the earth and creating tremendous changes in all life on the planet during this specific period of time. You are living in a most exciting era. This is a period of major transition. Due to these new energies, humanity as a whole will rise to its next level of development. This rise in consciousness has special challenges as many of you are not aware of what is happening and may be feeling confused.

Your awakening process—and that of humanity as a whole—is guided by present and future changes in the energies on earth. If you are aware of these changes, your growth process will be much easier. You will be able to live your life with far less struggle.

You can learn to be aware of the new energies and use them for your higher good

Due to the new energies, earth changes are occurring in the visible, ordinary reality in which you live as well as in the spiritual reality that underlies your ordinary reality. These energies come from the spiritual realms and cannot be perceived with your ordinary senses. Indeed, your ordinary senses reflect only a small part of the true, multidimensional reality of the universe.

However, behind your ordinary senses you have a different set of senses that we may call your inner senses. When you learn to sense behind your senses, so to speak, you develop your inner senses. With these inner senses you are perfectly able to perceive the spiritual realms and the earth changes that are occurring at these levels.

Many energies from the universe affect the earth plane. You are only beginning to recognize the existence of these energies. Most of you are familiar with radio waves and with the forces of electricity, but you cannot yet perceive a whole range of much more subtle energies. These subtle energies influence consciousness on earth in all its aspects.

Consciousness, as you will learn to see, is much more than the thoughts you have. Every form on your planet, in its essence, consists of Divine Consciousness. So even a rock or a drop of water contains Divine Consciousness. Plants and all the cells of your body have a consciousness of their own. Human consciousness is the highest form of consciousness on the earth plane.

However, while you are on the earth plane as a human being, you have only a small part of the consciousness of your whole being available to you.

Only part of your being is incarnated on earth. Your life on the earth plane is a fascinating school due to the limitations set by the specific conditions on earth. These limitations, however, may cause you much confusion as they greatly limit your perception.

Your life is meant to be joyful

You are wonderful, loving beings of love and light. Due to the density of the energies on the earth plane that create reality as you perceive it, there is much unknowingness in every one of you about your true nature and your true mission on earth. You all came here with a specific reason and purpose. All of you have forgotten why you incarnated at this specific time and what your purpose in this life is.

The denser energies of the earth plane create the illusion of time and space as well as the illusion of the existence of a material world. You are so enchanted by these illusions that you find it difficult to see behind them. You may have heard about advanced masters in the Himalayas who are able to manifest themselves in more than one location simultaneously, levitate, live without food, and even overcome death. In their lives they demonstrate that it is possible to see behind the illusions of three-dimensional reality. With these feats the masters demonstrate that reality as you perceive it is just an illusion and that you are captured in a dream.

In this book we will illuminate the illusions of your perception and teach you how to begin to transcend them. You will learn to see and sense your world as energy and to be able to adapt to the big energy changes on earth.

You need not be a slave to the circumstances of your earth. By knowing and working with energy, you can choose to live with joy and inner peace, helping humanity to make a smooth transition to its next level of growth.

Be joyful and peaceful amidst seeming chaos

The changes in the energies that come to the earth are increasing in their intensity as are the energies themselves. You may notice this, for example, in the way technology is developing in an almost exponential way. At the same time, there are developments that may eventually lead to the destruction of the earth. Politicians do not seem to have the power to stop this process. Many of you are feeling powerless or fearful about the future of humanity and the earth.

The great confusion and the many negative occurrences in the world today exist because most of you are not yet sensitive enough to perceive the changes in energy on earth.

The solution to these problems will come with the development of consciousness. Some of the problems humanity is facing now are actually the result of this rapidly increasing consciousness. With this increase, humanity as a whole will move on to its next level of growth and be able to handle the big problems of the earth. At this time, however, many of you are still not evolved enough to apply your growth in consciousness to the benefit of all and to solving the earth's problems.

One of our goals is to make you more sensitive to these earth changes and to develop your intuition and your ability to open to the guidance of your soul. This helps you to become more sensitive to the changes in energy on earth and to handle them effectively. Instead of living in fear and struggle or retreating from earth plane life, you are able to grow and flourish in the midst of the chaos and confusion which seem present now. You become a beacon of light for yourself and for others, helping humanity make a smooth transition to its next level of consciousness.

You chose to incarnate during a period of transformation

The more people there are who awaken to their higher consciousness, the more human consciousness will evolve in its intended direction. You live in a period of transition, a fascinating time which provides great opportunities to learn and to grow. This is why so many souls are choosing to incarnate at this time. The large number of people incarnating is in itself a major challenge to all humanity seeking a balanced way to create a good life on the earth for all.

You might think that your individual contribution is so small that the impact on the earth plane level will be hardly noticeable. This, however, is a distortion of your thoughts, created by the dense energy conditions of consciousness on the earth plane. Every one of you is a powerful spiritual being, able to contribute much more than you are actually aware of.

We send out a call to you to awaken to the divine, conscious being that you really are. The fact that you are reading this material, whether you bought this book or got it as a present, indicates that you are ready to make this quantum leap. No matter how you think or feel about yourself on the personality level, your soul is directing you on your spiritual path. You have heard and answered the call of your soul.

Your soul invites you to awaken to your higher path

It matters not whether you have just started your awakening process or you have already been on a spiritual path for a long time. We speak to all of you. We speak to you with our words, and at the same time, we transmit energy to you through these words in order to touch the deeper levels of your being so as to help you in your awakening.

Those of you who are already on a spiritual path know that there is no way back. The process of awakening brings so much joy and fulfillment into your life that you may have wondered why you did not choose to follow a spiritual path much earlier. It really may seem that you have awakened from a state of sleep.

The spiritual path is a process of self-realization, of awakening to your highest potential. This process can result in a fully developed consciousness.

Your life starts to work in better and better ways. You feel more secure about yourself and your relationships, and the quality of your work improves. Most important, however, is your increasing connection with your soul and with the Divine.

As you awaken, you also discover your life purpose. If your mission is to help humanity make a smooth transition to its next level of consciousness, you may choose to work in the earth reality itself. However, many of you choose to work on raising the consciousness of humanity by doing meditations or by praying.

You are not alone

All of you are connected with each other at the higher levels of your being. At this time, most of you are not aware of these connections. When you awaken to your true self, you become more and more aware of these connections and of the Oneness of which you are all part.

When you recognize these connections and learn to work with energy, you are able to assist many others in the development of their consciousness. You may choose to take a role in the forefront of the development of your own and humanity's consciousness. You will become more sensitive to energy changes on earth that are occurring right now and learn to handle them. The confusion that earth plane life may have created for you will gradually dissolve.

We ascended masters are filled with joy because you have chosen this path. It is our divine mission to assist you and all of humanity in raising your consciousness to the next levels. Our love for you is tremendous. If you could be aware of only one spark of the love that we have for you and that God has for you, your own heart would be overflowing with joy and bliss this very moment.

We are aware of you as you read this. We notice your energy vibration, and we joyfully and lovingly transmit energies of love and support to you. If it pleases you to do so, stop reading now and open yourself to our love. Inhale deeply and imagine how Divine Love spreads through your body.

We hope and expect that the lessons in this book will give you insights and inspiration for your own holy mission on the earth plane.

Our aim is to guide you to the realization of your true being

In the first part of this book, we intend to provide illumination about the way earth plane reality is constructed and how you function in it. As you acquire deeper insight into the nature of your reality and the way your consciousness works, you will develop the foundation you need to transcend the limitations of earth plane life.

In the second part of the book, we will suggest how you can create a life that heightens your awareness and expands your consciousness. By following these suggestions, you can begin to transcend ordinary reality and move smoothly through the energy shifts which are part of the earth's changes.

The third part of the book describes how the Divine Forces operate on your earth.

We remind you to always remember the greatness of your being. Thoughts about your not being important or worthy are illusions that are created by the specific circumstances of earth plane life with its limited scope of perception.

You can awaken to your true self and be the happiest person you can imagine.

For now, we say good-bye to you with all our love and light.

PART 1
Earth Changes

1.
Setting the Energy: Opening to the Higher Light

Bunny Flats to Panther Meadows

The following March we returned to Mount Shasta. Most of the mountain was still covered with snow. During our first hike, Phylos started talking after a few minutes.

Welcome, this is Phylos.

We suggest that those of you who are reading this material sit quietly in a comfortable position and relax as you read.

First, we want to welcome our channels, Jeroen and Froukje, who responded to our call and invitation to visit us here in order to receive some new information about the energy changes on earth and about our realms. Mount Shasta is a special place where our realms connect with the earth dimension. Here our dimension touches the dimension of your reality.

We ask our channels to walk while they are channeling. This makes it easier for us to get a steady stream of consciousness flowing from our realms to the realms of the earth plane. We use our channels to transmit our energies and light to humanity and to deliver information. This flow is also reaching out to everyone who reads this material. I, Phylos, am conscious right now of you who are reading this. Because you are reading this, you are one of the people who responded to our invitation to help us with the major shift in energy which humanity is making right now.[3]

We suggest that you who are reading this material sit quietly for a moment to set the energy for our teachings. In order to open your energy, we would like you to relax a bit more. Feel our special transmission of light from the slopes of Mount Shasta to you. Feel your body relaxing. Let all your muscles relax: your toes, your hips. Move your awareness upward through your body. Let your stomach be soft.

Open your chest and breathe a bit more deeply, finding our energies with every breath you take. Relax even more as you exhale, relaxing your shoulders, your head, and opening up the area around your neck. Let the skin of your forehead be soft, and relax your eyes and jaws. Open the top of your head, and imagine there is a light coming in through the top. Feel the stream of light come in, making you feel comfortable and safe.

Know that you are protected. Even if you sometimes feel as if you are alone, know that we are with you. We beings of light are helping you for your own benefit and for that of humanity. We are teaching you lessons because you are here with a purpose. We are helping you to rediscover that purpose since most of you lost your connection to it when you came to the earth with its denser energies.

When you were a little child, you still knew your reasons for coming here, knew that there would be help all the way through. The time has come to open the memory of your connection with our realms again and allow the stream of higher consciousness to help you to open the memory of who you truly are.

Find the energy around your body. You may see it or feel

it. As the light continues to pour in through the top of your head, notice the energies streaming around your body. This light spreads through your body, lighting up the energies around you, charging them with new energies which you may see as moving patterns.

Bring your awareness to the slow movement of these patterns, which we are now energizing. See how particles of light clear up the energy around you.

See how they move away slowly and easily, a calm and constant movement of patterns and maybe colors, making the patterns of light around you more complete.

Feel your connection with the earth. Feel how the energy of the soul of the earth carries you. At the same time, feel your connection with our realms. Feel how you are carried by our light and love.

Imagine that you are on Mount Shasta right now. It is not important whether you know this place or not. Just imagine that you are here. Sense that there is an easy stream of consciousness from the realms of the earth to our realms and back. Here time splits away from matter, allowing you to make a major leap forward to raise your vibration.

You may feel as if you are becoming lighter, as if you are moving up, while at the same time you are staying centered and connected to the earth. Hold these two perspectives at once now. Both perspectives are reinforcing each other. The higher you go, the more expanded your consciousness becomes, and the more grounded into the earth you feel.

Feel your connection to the soul of the earth carry you higher, expanding your consciousness.

In this more expanded state of being, you can ask me, Phylos, for whatever you want. You may also ask other masters, or your guides, your higher self, or maybe God. You may ask for insight, health, abundance, or whatever comes into your mind that you would like to receive right now. While we transmit to you, take some time to just be quiet and hold in your awareness whatever you are asking for.

Then come back slowly to your own energy. Find the center of your being, the part of you that has always been there and that knows who you really are. Enjoy the physical ease and harmony. Come back slowly, feeling your body more and more.

You had a glimpse into the harmony and light, the love and easy flow, the manifestations, and the abundance of our realms. You may have gained some insights about what you asked for. Maybe you also had glimpses of your purpose on earth as we transmitted the energy of this purpose to you too. Your life purpose is the mission that you have come to fulfill, that mission which gives you joy and happiness.

The fulfillment of your life purpose is always connected with feelings of joy, harmony, and peace. The fulfillment of your life purpose is definitely not connected with that inner voice that tells you in a negative way what you should or must do.

At this time, I, Phylos, wish you a most pleasant day or night. Know that any time you wish to feel the connection with us you may sit down quietly, relax your body, and ask for assistance. You may do this just because you feel like it or because you want to feel more in the flow. Know that I, Phylos, and many others in our realms are available to you and happy to assist you if you ask.

For now, we say good-bye to you with all our love and light.

2. Visit To Castle Lake: The Lemurians

Castle Lake, Mount Shasta

We were at Castle Lake, a beautiful, clear mountain lake near Mount Shasta. At that time we did not yet know that it was a highly spiritual place. Phylos had announced that he wanted to open up our energies more here in order to help us gain more trust in our ability to receive images and information.

Welcome, this is Phylos. You are about to enter a very ancient sacred place in which we want to teach Froukje to trust the images she is receiving.

***

P: Now, Froukje, close your eyes and concentrate on your inner senses, connecting with the energy of this spot, with the light from above, and with us ascended masters. Just start describing what you see, feel, or hear.

F: I see a point of light and I see water.

P: Listen to the sounds of the water. Concentrate on the water and listen to what it tells you. Identify anything that is there for you.

F: I see a waterfall.

P: What do you see at the waterfall?

F: Some kind of rainbow.

P: Concentrate on the rainbow. It does not matter if you

see other images. Just describe what you are seeing. These images may be very brief.

F: I see bubbles of some kind. They grow in size as they take on the colors of the rainbow. Eventually they burst. I see a figure in a globe. The globe has a steering wheel. The figure looks like a child's drawing, with a very thin body. I also see a little cart with a handle for steering. The cart makes movements in the air. It lifts upward, then somersaults into space toward the light, then floats back down again.

P: Okay. What do you see on the ground?

F: I see a round spot surrounded by a radiant glow. This appears to be a hole in the earth. One can enter this hole. An elevator goes down the hole.

P: All right, and what is underneath?

F: A corridor and a system of caves.

P: All right. If you wish, you can move your consciousness further into this corridor and system of caves, or perhaps you can move your consciousness up to your body again.

F: The same way?

P: Yes.

F: I will move up again now.

P: In an instant, you may be back on the spot where we started in your earth dimension. Listen to the sound of the water again. Now simply concentrate on the same spot again, including in your awareness the area that surrounds it. Then describe what you see here, what has been here. Trust your images.

F: I see a woman, an Indian woman.

P: All right, tell more. Take this picture and go on from there. What is she doing? What is happening?

F: She is looking over the water, washing her face. There

are tents. She is going to hunt on a horse, with a bow and arrow.

While Phylos worked with Froukje, I suddenly heard some fierce cries coming from the rocks at the other side of the lake. I was alarmed.

P: For your information, Jeroen just shivered because he very clearly heard the sound of yelling Native Americans on the mountains here. He opened his eyes, thinking someone was here. There are, in fact, spirits present which you can hear if you concentrate on them. Do not worry, there is no reason for fear. We guided you both here in order to acquaint you with a deeper level of reality so that you could learn to see and hear all kinds of energies. You are safe and protected so do not fear whatever you see or hear. Just go on now.

F: I see Native Americans dancing around something with beautiful, circular movements. There are men with drums also. Now I see a medicine woman who is treating a woman in a tent. Or maybe she is embalming her, I don't know for sure.

P: All right, go a bit further in time. Leave these images and go on. What is at this spot?

F: A bird, a bird of prey.

P: What is it doing, what is it seeing?

F: It is flying over the lake.

P: Watch through the eyes of the bird.

F: It sees a UFO arriving and landing. Now through the bird's eyes, I see the UFO landing. The UFO is a greenish light. Some creatures are coming out of it, greenish creatures. They seem to be marking something on the ground with a stone. A round spot, a circle of light. Now it seems that this circle can disconnect from the earth. In fact, the circle appears to be a kind of tube.

P: Now as you leave these images, know that you have just seen some events that actually occurred on this spot. You may read about them in the booklet that you just bought but have not yet read.[4] One of the things you saw was an elevator in the corridors in the Lemurian time. This spot is an opening to outer space. This opening still exists. However, the spot is not visible and is impossible to find because a slight shift in dimension has been created here in order to prevent anyone from finding the entrance.

You also saw images of the Native Americans who lived in this area, coming here to celebrate special events. The crying that Jeroen heard was related to killings that happened on the other side of the lake. You have also found the UFO landing spot.

Froukje, you may read about this in the booklet you just bought, and of course when you do, you will get a strong affirmation that what you have seen is not just imagination. It is based on facts. That is what we wanted to show you.

Now you can both return to your present time and reality. Feel the center of your being, your connection to the earth here, and again, please realize that this spot is a very ancient and powerful one. If you open yourself up to these energies, just being here can help you to heal and energize. If you are feeling humble, that is all right. The power of this spot is beyond anything you have yet encountered.

For now, we say good-bye to you with all our love and light. You can have some time to enjoy this place and maybe pick up images and sounds of ancient voices. Again, do not fear what you may see or hear. All these experiences are given to you for learning. The voices and images were shown to you because the spirits of this place are helpful and enjoy being helpful. They are here right now.

EARTH CHANGES

After a break, we started to walk upward on the left side of the lake, on a steep trail leading high above the lake. Our view of the lake from above Mount Shasta was magnificent. While we walked upward, Phylos started talking again.

Welcome, this is Phylos. You both did very well today.

Now we will give you some information about this Castle Lake area. At the present time, this spot continues to be an entrance into the corridors within the mountain. However, it is no longer a major entrance. The corridors Froukje saw underneath the surface of the earth are Lemurian.

In a way, the Lemurian civilization still exists today, but the whole civilization has shifted slightly in dimension. It is still in a dimension very close to your earth dimension but just slightly within another reality. This effectively prevents your earth civilization from detecting this civilization. Your methods are not yet advanced enough to do so.

This ancient Lemurian civilization hides itself for many reasons. It still exists on the earth for the purpose of helping people find their true destination during this time of earth changes. In order to help you to find this destination, the Lemurians are helping to change some of the denser energies on the earth plane.

All people on the earth originally came from different places: you are all people from the stars. In this area, people who came from the Pleiades live. Other people from other star systems also live here.

People have come from the stars into the denser energy systems of the earth to experience the earth's beauty and its system of dimensions. The earth has four dimensions[5] and an additional fifth dimension that is a transition point to our dimension. On the earth, people have a good opportunity to learn and to evolve highly spiritual qualities like harmony, beauty, co-operation, and joy.

The density of the energies on the earth results in the development of the denser human qualities such as hate, aggression, greed, and jealousy. These are the counterparts of the beautiful soul qualities, such as beauty, love, and harmony.

Since the consciousness of humanity is still expanding in an unbalanced way, the unavoidable result is the development of these denser qualities. They have become very strong now because you as a race are not caring enough for the earth; you are exploiting it.

We ascended masters need to be in dimensions that are not affected by the denser energies so that we can help bring about the necessary shifts and balances in your growth. That is why at this moment the Lemurians, as well as we ascended masters, have stepped back a little. In this way, we will not be affected by the denser energies that are preoccupying humanity right now. Since we have adjusted our energy slightly to be able to assist you, we are able to stay in our pure state of love and joy.

We advise you not to climb higher now. You have reached a point where going on much further would be physically dangerous for you. So you might prefer to return to your campsite now.

For now, we say good-bye to you with all our love and light.

3.
The Personality and Its Presence on Earth

Indian Springs, Castle Crags

Welcome, this is Phylos.

As you arrive on the top of this hill, we suggest that you walk a little further, right between those trees to a power spot there. Good. Now notice how you can feel the energy of the earth and the power of the rocks in front of you.

We sat down on the spot that Phylos had identified and stayed there for a while. We enjoyed the smooth, soft energy that seemed to vibrate from the earth. Huge pinecones, bigger than we had ever seen before, were all over the place.

While you walk, we will tell a bit more about the personality and its presence on the earth.

We have taken you here to awaken memories of this sacred place. You, Froukje, once dwelled here. Earlier the guides said that you had no Native American incarnations. I am telling you now that you did. Moreover, you had more than one.

As you walk on this holy ground, every step you take brings a bit more of your memory from another self into your consciousness. As you are walking, you may remember that you have been in this place before. Memories may also come back to you later in dreams. The views of this environment, which you find breathtaking, will help you to awaken your old memories.

Your self is divided into several parts

Your true self is divided into several parts. When you incarnate on the earth, only one or two of these parts incarnate at a time. At least one part of your true self stays in the higher dimensions. Another part stays on the star from which you came. From there it sends life-force energy to your being on the earth and awakens your vision. After you die, each of the selves takes its learning experiences from this particular lifetime back to the one or more other selves that exist on other levels of reality.

Most of the time, a self that incarnates on the earth plane will do so repeatedly in order to finish its projects and collect all the information it wants.

The guides said that you had not incarnated as a Native American. This was true about only one self, the self that you are right now. At this sacred spot, it is possible to cross the lines between the selves and to make the memories of one self available to another self in the earth dimension.

With every step you take here, you can awaken more of these memories. In this way, you bring the energy of the memories together. On an energetic level, you bring together the DNA of these selves.

All channelings have distortions

Some channeled books say that strands were taken away from your DNA during some war by beings with bad intentions. However, that is a misconception. Such stories are distortions which can occur easily because those who channel are human beings who live in accordance with the physical laws of the earth—where some distortions in channeled material are inevitable.

In order for you to survive in the earthly dimensions, you must split off from your completeness. This splitting gives rise to many distortions in your perceptions, in your thoughts about reality, and in what you are able to channel from higher sources.

Do not think that what you are channeling right now is the only truth! It is only part of the truth, just as information that other channels are bringing through is only part of the truth and partly distorted.

You may find that different channeled materials seem to contain contradictory views about reality.

This is why it is so important that many people channel. Since you are intelligent beings, one of your tasks is to find the true essence of these materials. When I say that you are intelligent, I am not speaking about intelligence as it is usually understood, which is exclusively about intellectual capacities. I am speaking about a more powerful intelligence, one which comes from your intuition.

We use many channels in order to give you a complete picture.

Your understanding of reality may be distorted because you are living in a world of divisions such as the division between good and evil. Seen from a higher level, these divisions are illusions, which develop because of the way earth plane reality is constructed. This division between good and evil may give rise to distorted stories. This is evident in many channeled stories about UFOs. These are often unconsciously inspired by science fiction. Unfortunately, such distortions in channeling are hard to avoid because a channel has to translate our abstract information into the words and sentences of the human mind.

Divisions exist in our dimensions too. These divisions are at a much higher level than yours, and they are beyond judgment. We have to translate our material from a much more abstract and multidimensional energy level to your level of thinking which uses divisions. The divisions that we make when we speak about masters, angels, and other entities are the way we attempt to translate our more abstract information to your world of divisions. We beings of light do not have concrete forms. Were we only to say, "God is all there is," we would in essence be telling the truth. But many dimensions are involved in this truth. In order to make things comprehensible to you, we have to divide our information into bits and work with entities.

Your complete self has twelve strands of DNA

Now back to the DNA story. Your complete self does, indeed, have twelve strands of DNA. When you come back to our dimensions, you will find the "lost" strands of DNA. Because humanity is making an important shift now, it is important for you in your existence on the earth to begin to reestablish contact with your other selves and to make your DNA more complete on a spiritual level. Especially the chosen ones will benefit from meditation and from making contact with their complete selves and their complete DNA at a spiritual level. The chosen ones are those who are in the front line, helping to prepare humanity for the big shift in consciousness that is coming and has, in fact, already begun.

EARTH CHANGES

At the personality level, this contact makes it possible for you to change the spiritual, political, and material circumstances on the earth.

This is the end of our first chapter.

***

P: You had a question, Froukje?

F: You talk about the different selves. Is this the same as saying that your soul has different personalities?

P: Indeed, you could say that all your selves together are a major part of your soul. Your soul is also active in dimensions that are so far away from what the selves are doing that for practical purposes we would not call those parts of the soul "selves." If, however, you would prefer to do so, you might. Some parts of your soul are in rocks, or in trees, or in other star-systems. You might say that in a way these are selves too.

F: How about twin-souls? And what about my friend who says she is one of "quintuple-souls?"

P: The concept of twin-souls and triple-souls, and so on, refers to the selves, but it is an example of how you in your reality interpret our information too literally. As we translate our information into your world of divisions, we have to adapt all the information so you can understand it. When you interpret it too literally, it often no longer reflects its true essence. Often people interpret systems of information that were given at another time too literally. Astrology is an example of such a system.

Throughout history, some people have understood new concepts, which made their way into earth plane consciousness. However, over time, people began to interpret the information too literally. They applied it to daily life and developed rules of behavior from the original teachings. Therefore, the information is now distorted and no longer reflects the truth. This process of distorting the truth occurred in the past and still occurs today.

This is why we always have to go on teaching. When you say that you met your twin-soul, you are offering a literal, but not quite true, perspective on how things really are.

For now, we say good-bye to you with all our love and light. We hope to continue our teachings at another other time.

Our visit to the mountain had come to an end. This was the end of our first encounter with Phylos's teachings on Mount Shasta. We would not be back until summer.

4. Why Write This Book?

Squaw Meadow, Mount Shasta

Welcome, this is Phylos. We welcome you back to these holy grounds of Mount Shasta. We have been working on your energies for quite a while now and we are glad that you have both taken some big steps in your growth. You can hold more light now. This will deepen the quality of our transmissions and the purity of the information that will come through.

We suggest that you sit down for a while before we start giving you information. Connect with the energies here and harmonize with them. When you look up at the mountain, pause for a while, and connect with its energy.

Thus far, we had not taken much time to enjoy our return to Mount Shasta. After registering as visitors at the registration booth in the parking lot, we turned our tape recorder on and began our climb. Almost immediately, Phylos spoke his welcoming words. We were very close to the place where he had so unexpectedly started talking to us a year ago.

When we sat down, we focused on the beautiful energy of the mountain. The quiet here was amplified by the nasal kra-a-a sound of the birds which we had also spotted here last year. After consulting a book about North American birds, we had concluded that these birds were Clark's Nutcrackers. We also enjoyed the beautiful little orange chipmunks. Sitting on these slopes filled us with great joy and a sense of fulfillment. After about fifteen minutes, Phylos resumed the dictation.

Good. You did very well in adapting your energies, in getting into the flow of the energy of the mountain and of our energies. Now we will continue with the book. This chapter will discuss our reasons for writing this book.

The purpose of our speaking through you is to give information about the energies on the earth plane, the evolution of humanity, the conditions in which you as humans live on the earth, your purpose in being here, and how to live well.

Although we ascended masters have already given you a lot of material in the past, we find it necessary to speak again because this material has a certain fluidity. This means that you cannot apply the teachings of many years ago to the situation of today. There have been major energy shifts on the earth plane as well as major shifts in the mass thinking of humanity.

Earth changes influence the consciousness of humanity

Every time we speak, we adjust our information to the energy and the mass thinking of the time. This does not mean that mass thinking is right. It is only a reflection of the mean level of development of humanity at any given stage. Changes in the level of consciousness of humanity are a direct result of changes in the energies that are coming to the earth plane.

In the early years of the twentieth century, mass thinking was linear and based on polarities and other divisions. During this period, the mental energy body developed quickly.[6] At the same time, human consciousness was rising to a level where humanity was able to grasp more of the insights of higher consciousness.

For our information to be understood by humanity at that time, we had to address mainly the mental energy body of human beings. Therefore a lot of teachings from the masters were about hierarchies in your earth plane and in our realms.

When the mental energy body is not balanced with the emotional and intuitive energy bodies, the linear and hierarchical way in which it operates may result in unbalanced ideas and forms. Hence the rise of racism. It is true that many great scientific developments came out of the quick development of the mental energy body as well, but they too were often unbalanced and not in harmony with human values or the environment. We will discuss this more later.

Due to the new energies coming to the earth plane, humanity is making another shift now. During the years after the Second World War, there was a major development of the emotional energy body. This is still going on today. Now the shift toward the development of the intuitive energy body is starting. In fact, it has already started, but the major part of this development is yet to come.

Forms are loosening.

The new energies coming to earth plane also accelerate the speed at which forms change. This concerns forms in your outer world as well as forms at the energy levels.

You can already feel and see how forms are loosening when you observe the changes in computer communications and the development of virtual reality. This loosening of forms and boundaries will continue in ways that you cannot imagine right now.

First, forms will begin to loosen on an energy level. Their energy patterns will change more and more rapidly. Initially, this will influence your intuitive, emotional, and mental energy bodies. Later, this will also affect your physical body.

As a result of this, mental concepts will be more fluid and will change more quickly, and emotions will come and go more quickly. Later, the physical body will become more fluid and have fewer of the circumscribed boundaries that you now perceive. This will occur at a later stage because the denser the level of energy, the more time it takes to make the changes.

However, you can already see the early stages of this process of the loosening of your body's boundaries. This phenomenon becomes apparent when you explore the energy fields which exist beyond your physical body. Sensing these energies is far easier at this time than it was ten years ago.

The boundaries of the human energy bodies are already dissolving. Many people are experiencing this in meditation. The denser parts of the physical body will begin to become less defined during a later stage.

People who have difficulty keeping a fluid mind and fluid emotions will find this to be a difficult time. The linear and hierarchical patterns of the mental energy body are no longer appropriate; great flexibility and adaptation to the rapid changes are necessary. Some people may cling too tightly to the benefits of the development of the mental energy body and the luxuries and tools that have come from that. Some people may have become too rigid in their over emphasis of the importance of emotions and their role in personal growth. This is evident in some psychotherapeutic disciplines and growth movements. Humanity's next level of growth involves developing its intuitive energy body. People will need to become more fluid and more flexible in order to complete this process.

Eventually the more solid, denser forms of your earth plane will also start to dissolve. Here on Mount Shasta you see these rocks all about you that look and feel very solid. However, we tell you that in reality this solidity is an illusion. You make a big effort to climb these illusions, but from our perspective they are illusions indeed! From our perspective, these rocks are not solid at all. I can make my consciousness as small or as large as I want, and I can travel as easily through these rocks as through air.

Consciousness knows no boundaries. In your world, the way in which you perceive gives you the impression that things are solid and distinct from one another. All you perceive is a manifestation of consciousness as it is focused into the special conditions of the earth. We will elaborate on this in later chapters. For now, what is important is that you know that the world as you perceive it is not the way it really is. What I am telling you about the changes that are happening is not revolutionary at all because it is how reality is, always has been, and always will be. As humanity grows into its next stages and as your consciousness expands, you will be more and more able to see how the strong, new energies on earth dissolve the existing forms.

In order to develop its intuitive energy body, humanity will require fluidity and the capacity to let go of forms that now seem very fixed. This process of developing of the intuitive energy body signifies a period of higher consciousness for humanity.

At the end of this chapter, we will guide you into a meditation so that our words are not just intellectual food for your mental body, but that they will also give you an intuitive sense of what we mean.

We will end this chapter with a few remarks about our being here on Mount Shasta.

These days, we ascended masters no longer appear in physical forms. People can no longer find the doorway to our place in the mountain because we have shifted our energies slightly outside of your reality. We are still very close in order to guide you, but now you will not find us in a physical form. We had to do this because the energies on the earth plane are becoming less dense and the forms are loosening. The energies are quite chaotic and sometimes disturbing to us.

In order to keep a clear focus of light on your development, we have to create a bit more distance between humanity and ourselves than we used to. However, when your development reaches a point where the energies are less chaotic, there may be a time when we will appear physically again.

This is the end of this chapter. For now, we say good-bye to you with all our love and light.

5.

Meditation: Expanding through the Physical Boundary

Squaw Meadows

Welcome, this is Phylos.

1. Imagine that you are in a beautiful meadow. You can feel the sun on your skin. Maybe there is a slight breeze. There are beautiful flowers and there is a nice little stream of water. You can hear the sounds of birds and insects. You may feel a perfect harmony between yourself and this beautiful place.

As you inhale, you breathe in the energy of this beautiful, sacred spot. Let the energy float through your body. Imagine that you are breathing in light. The light flows through your body and lights up every part of your organs, your bones, your nerves, and your skin. Your whole body radiates the beautiful energy of the meadow. Light comes into your cells, molecules, and atoms.

2. Make yourself so small that you can place your awareness into one cell. Become that cell now. You are in that cell; see the molecules and the atoms alive in that cell. The cell wall surrounds you. Feel the stream of light that is coming in now. Feel the joy and the love in this light, and feel how it revitalizes you.

Become even smaller now. You are now inside a molecule.

See the nucleus and the atoms of the molecule, and again feel the light coming in.

3. You can easily travel from one molecule to another. You can move slowly or move faster and faster. Travel now through the molecules, and see the atoms and the electrons moving in beautiful patterns. You can slow down the pace at which the atoms and electrons move so you can observe them better, or you can speed up so much that you are at the same pace as the speed of the electrons.

You feel free. Just let yourself flow on the forces of the atoms that you can feel now. You move freely through the atoms, not only of one cell, but of all cells, billions of cells. You are in a world now where you can perceive the patterns of light and energy. You are free, and you feel the energy streams upon which you can ride.

4. You can travel through your whole body, and you can move out of it. There really is no boundary, there are just the same structures of atoms, and of electrons. There may be differences in how you feel when you are inside or outside of your body, but being the size of an electron you can move in and out freely. There really is no boundary. There really is no body. There is only light, and beautiful patterns of movement. You can see that all atoms and electrons move and are not solid at all.

5. Now become larger again, back to your normal proportions, and feel your body as you sit now. Feel the boundary of your body and feel how that boundary feels. How do you know that the boundary of your body is a boundary? Can you describe it? How do you know where your boundary is? How do you perceive where your boundary is when your eyes are closed?

Imagine that your body is expanding, maybe just an inch

in all directions. Your boundary is moving one inch out. Move one inch out beyond every part of your body: your feet, your legs, your torso, your arms, your hands, your neck, and your head.

Now go five inches out, and still feel where your boundary is. And now feel your boundary ten inches beyond your body, and then move out thirty inches from your body. As you do so, you may start to feel that you are moving into a bubble of light. As you expand further out now, maybe three feet out, feel your boundary, feel yourself in a bubble of light which extends three feet out.

6. Imagine that you do not feel the normal boundaries of your body anymore. If you feel some itching or discomfort, make your bubble larger.

Now also let the boundary of the bubble dissolve, and feel yourself moving out in all directions. Feel that you can grow larger and larger, not just a few feet larger, but much, much larger. You become as large as the earth and even larger. See the earth becoming a molecule in your body as you become as large as the whole universe.

7. After some time, let yourself become smaller again, and come back to your normal size.

Still with your eyes closed, sense your present surroundings. Where do you sense space, and where do you sense obstacles? Do you sense colors, or light? Notice that you have the ability to sense outside of your body.

8. Now make the area that you sense much larger. If you are in a room, expand your awareness outside of the room, outside of the building. Sense an area that is about a mile around you. Notice that you can pick up the energy a mile away in all directions. Stay in this circle extending about a mile beyond you, and see if you can find a spot within it that attracts your attention.

Bring all your awareness to that spot, and place the center of your perception on that spot. Look around you now. What do you see? How does it feel? Maybe you can discover why it attracted your attention.

9. After you have experienced this for a while, gently bring your awareness back to the place where you are sitting, coming back to your normal consciousness, and back into your body.

We say good-bye to you with all our love and light.

6.
The Nature of Consciousness and Its Layers

Lake Helen Ascension, Mount Shasta

Welcome, this is Phylos.

As we told you yesterday, humanity is making a big shift toward the development and use of the intuitive energy body because consciousness in itself is ever-expanding and ever-growing. This shift is happening in a wave like fashion.

Consciousness grows in spiraling waves

This process of development contains important waves of growth and decline. After every decline, the next growth wave picks up at a higher level, so it would be more accurate to speak of a spiraling movement in growth. One person's birth, lifetime, and death might be considered a small spiral. The rise and decline of a whole species or of an entire civilization, such as that of Atlantis or Lemuria, might be considered a big wave or spiral.

There are all kinds of layers in consciousness. The organization of your civilization is reflected in the level of consciousness of your society. Your civilization now is not at the level of consciousness once enjoyed by the civilizations of Atlantis and Lemuria, but you are at a point where your consciousness is expanding and growing in an exponential way.

The emergence or decline of forms also happens in waves or spirals. When a civilization declines, existing forms disappear and new forms emerge. Two major cycles of growth and decline are happening in your world right now. The first is that of the expansion of consciousness along with the development of the intuitive energy body. The second is the exponential growth of forms. This process has almost peaked now and reached the point at which the forms will begin to decline.

The forms of your civilization are still growing, but they are on the verge of decline. Do not ask us to say precisely when the decline will begin. It may become noticeable and begin to affect your lives about thirty or fifty years from now.

As consciousness is not yet expanding in such a way as to help forms decline in a smooth way, there is a risk that the decline could happen in quite an explosive way. Humanity, which created these forms, cannot control this.

Increasing the use of your intuition will prevent disasters

The development of the mental energy body has resulted in many forms on the earth. These forms seem to have taken over human life on the earth. They are caught up in a process of their own, a process which is difficult to stop.

Meanwhile, the development of the intuitive energy body is still in its beginning stages.

Humanity could prevent disasters by using intuition, but humanity has not yet progressed to this point. With your intuitive energy body, you are able to receive energies from the higher realms and translate them into insights. The decline of society and its forms could be explosive, hence dangerous. Insights from the higher realms will eventually help humanity find the wisdom and knowledge to deal effectively with this decline.

Thinking and decision-making will no longer come only from the mental energy body but will be guided by intuitive insights.

During the process of developing its intuitive body, humanity will get in touch with completely new dimensions of reality, dimensions that are almost inconceivable today.

These dimensions have great potential to find new ways of creating forms that have almost no physical boundaries. Further stages of the development of the intuitive energy body will result in new methods of transportation and other practical ways of improving life on the earth.

On one hand, many people today are awakening their consciousness. They are caring for their bodies and for the earth, eating more healthily, and exercising more than before. On the other hand, industry keeps producing more and more cars and other energy-consuming technologies which the earth will not be able to handle much longer.

One of the reasons we are grateful for people like you, who are holding a focus to let our energies come through, is that we can transmit and help spread the information that humanity now requires. This information will hasten the process of developing the intuitive energy body, facilitating a smoother and less dramatic transition.

The basic elements of consciousness are love, creativity, and intent

Now we will talk about the nature of consciousness and its layers.

The spiraling growth and decline of consciousness is happening on many levels and dimensions at once. For purposes of teaching, we will talk mainly about your plane of existence in the four dimensions of time and space. Keep in mind, however, that the same process is also happening in other dimensions outside your time and space, as well as in other dimensions of your own being. When you are able to perceive the patterns of these energies, you will see wonderful spiraling patterns, not only spiraling outward, but also spiraling inward into themselves.

There are three major forces contributing to the way consciousness expands and declines. The main force and basic energy is *love*. Indeed, it is the energy you can feel and perceive on your earth in the form of love. Aspects of that love energy are qualities like beauty and perfection. It is the kind of love you experience when you are in a beautiful place and feel love for the beauty and perfection of that environment.

The second major force of consciousness is *creativity*. This force causes the love energy of consciousness to create forms and patterns. These are created in your world and also in worlds outside yours. Creativity is an ever-expanding process, going on forever, always seeking newer, higher, and better forms.

The third main force operating in consciousness is *intent*, or will. Intent gives direction to the creativity so that the forms have meaning and purpose. When creativity is combined with love and intent, beautiful and meaningful patterns with a high degree of perfection emerge. Creating these patterns is a major aim of consciousness.

You are able to live in your world only because consciousness has imposed certain rules and limitations upon this environment, such as those inherent in the concepts of time and space. These rules and limitations create the illusion that Oneness can be divided into separate parts. The set of rules that creates your earth environment gives wonderful opportunities for consciousness to create beautiful forms. You are one such form.

At the same time these rules put limitations on how consciousness can operate in this environment. The more freely your consciousness moves within the limitations of these rules, the more you are in contact with love and Higher Will, and the more beautiful and perfect the forms you create will be. One of the major goals of your being on earth now is to reestablish the full potential of your contact with the love and Higher Will of the universe.

I am using the terms intent and Higher Will interchangeably. By *intent*, I mean the action of your will, that part of the Oneness that is you. By Higher Will, I mean the intent of the universe, of consciousness itself, of the Oneness.

Love, creativity and intent need to be balanced

The contact with love, creativity, and intent, which you are learning to reestablish, is far from perfect in most people because of the many restrictions inherent in the rules operating on the earth plane. One way for people to develop this contact is by meditating.

Since your contact with love and Higher Will is not perfect, not all the forms you create are perfect. If creativity is without love, you can create forms that do not have a higher meaning. Examples of such forms are weapons or chemicals that are not in harmony with the environment. They were created with a combination of creativity and intent, but their connection with love was far from perfect.

When there is creativity without intent, disasters may

occur even though love may be involved. Consider the beauty of a volcanic eruption, or a big flood, or a storm.

If creativity is missing, if there is only love and intent, there will be no development, no movement. You may see this in people who have idealistic ideas but who lack the creative resources to bring them into form.

You can speed up the development of your intuitive energy body

When you awaken your intuitive energy body, you connect more closely with these three forces of consciousness. Thus you can more easily create those forms that are closer to the beauty and perfection of your true being and more in harmony with Higher Will.

Awakening the intuitive energy body is a process that will occur automatically with the evolution of humanity. However, since the basic patterns already exist inside your DNA, it is possible for you to speed up this process. The way to do this is to meditate in order to develop your inner senses and to find the doorways to higher levels of being. In a later chapter, we will comment on the doorways to these higher levels.

Meditating is important. It is also important to open your energies to receive help from our realms. Many energies and beings in our realms have the ability to help you. They too have the intent to expand their consciousness. They are in close contact with the energy of love, and their creativity and love will help to open yours. Helping you expands their consciousness in return. When you help others, your consciousness expands in the same way.

How you perceive higher beings depends on your perception of these energies

EARTH CHANGES

Higher energies or entities may take many forms in your perception. What you see when you encounter a being of light or an extraterrestrial being is a combination of the energy of that being and the way your perceptual system interprets it. In other words, you create your perceptions of these energies. Most likely you will perceive them in forms that resemble human beings, although you might also see many auras around them. They may remind you of pictures of fairies or religious paintings of angels.

Usually you will see these beings with your inner eyes, but occasionally you may have visions of them in outer reality. Important to keep in mind is the fact that the form in which you perceive these beings is just one of the possible forms in which they may appear to you. These entities may appear to you as concrete forms, as light, or in even more abstract ways. If you see angels, dwarfs, or even gnomes, do not fear that you are just imagining them or tapping into a memory of pictures you once saw. Realize that people who had early glimpses of these beings created these pictures.

Perhaps you will enjoy knowing that many of the beings in your fairy tales are very real indeed. Some of these beings are quite close to your reality while others are very distant.

Maybe at this point you have some questions about extraterrestrial life. This does exist but in dimensions other than yours. When entities from other dimensions appear in your world, they take on forms that you may perceive in your special human ways. Realize, however, that what you see is not how they truly are. So do not take these images too literally. If you see three-fingered green beings with antennae on their heads, it does not mean that this is how they truly are. This may only be the way you perceive them with your senses.

We will guide you into a meditation now to assist you to call upon the ascended masters and open to receive our help.

7.
Meditation: Opening to Your Inner Being

Mount Shasta, lower slopes

Welcome, this is Phylos.

1. Imagine that you are on the slopes of Mount Shasta. Feel the high, fine, spiritual energy that is present, and connect with that energy.

Relax your body a bit more. Feel your contact with the earth. Relax your legs, your torso, your arms, your neck, your head, and your face. Draw all of your awareness inside yourself more and more. See if you can find a smaller and smaller point into which to draw your awareness. Draw it into the very core of your being.

2. There is a point inside you that is the connection point between you and other dimensions. Find that point now, and observe your body from there. Observe the volume and the boundaries of your body, and begin to see your body as energy. You may see patterns, colors, or structures.

See or imagine the energy of your body as light, extending just a few inches beyond the boundaries of your body. Perhaps you can see lines of light, vibrant intersecting lines of energy. Perhaps you think you are imagining it all. That is just fine.

3. Now expand your perception even beyond that. You may see some of the auras around your body. Maybe you can see colors, or movements. See how far you can move out

with your awareness in all directions. Look at the patterns, the colors. Maybe you see places where there is more light, and places where there is less light, or places where there are disturbances.

4. Imagine now that there is a line extending vertically from the top of your head. Through this line, energy flows into your head and out of your head. When you feel this flow, call upon the ascended masters of Mount Shasta. Ask the masters to connect with you and blend your energy with theirs. Ask the ascended masters for light, help, and support in the process of awakening your intuitive energy body. Ask them to open your third eye and to connect you with your guides and the energy of the masters.

Be quiet for a while and feel the energy of the masters come in. As their energy flows into your body and your energy field, you may or may not have physical sensations.

5. Ask the masters to help you go deeper into yourself, into the part of you that has knowledge beyond the knowledge you normally have about the earth. Get a feeling or a glimpse of that part of you. It may seem to be deep inside you. When you do this, your consciousness opens up more. This part knows about all the paths you have taken in the past, are taking now, and may take in the future.

6. Let the energy of Mount Shasta and the masters flow through you and take you to an even deeper layer. Feel your connection with the mountain, and feel yourself going deeper and deeper within. Find the reflection of the energy of the masters and of the mountain within your inner being. Find also the love, creativity, and intent in that reflection. Feel how these three aspects of your consciousness are amplified, as though your consciousness radiates love and creativity.

Places in your mind that were rigid now become flexible

again. You may perceive this as moving lines of light. It is as if energy is flowing through long unused pipelines. The light in your brain and in your mental body becomes more focused. Your whole body is vibrating with this enormous light which contains frequencies of the Higher Will.

7. Feel the peace that comes over you, a peace that comes over you when you surrender to the higher light.

Enjoy this state of being perfectly happy and of being completely in the now. Nothing bothers you; you just are—radiating love, and experiencing the fluidity of your mind, emotions, and body. Your organs, blood stream, and nerves are working together in smooth and harmonious ways.

You have connected your intent with the Higher Will. This connection has given you a peaceful, trusting feeling, and an inner knowing that every step you take serves your higher purpose.

8. Now sense the masters that are present as light. Maybe you can also sense other high beings that have assembled here in response to our call. They come to help you open your intuitive energy body even more.

Sense their presence, and be quiet for a while, receiving their transmissions of light and love.

9. Feel the bliss, and thank these high beings for what they have given you. Send them your love and light in return. Notice how grateful they are for your love and light. Say goodbye to these masters and beings, knowing that you can call upon them again at any time you wish.

10. Return to your own energy, becoming aware of your physical body in the earthly dimension again, feeling your legs, your torso, your arms, your head. Breathe in deeply, feeling connected to the earth. When you are ready, open your eyes and come back. Enjoy the rest of the day in the blissful, loving energy that you have just received.

For now, we say good-bye to you with all our love and light.

8.
Time and Space
Castle Lake—Heart Lake

Welcome, this is Phylos.

We welcome you back to Castle Lake, a place of very high energy indeed.

Although there are corridors of energy going from this place to Mount Shasta, this area is secluded and has a very high energy of its own. This makes it attractive to many high beings.

This chapter will deal with the way time and space interconnect.

The concepts of time and space are beyond your ability to grasp

Actually, time and space are just a set of rules that were created in order to facilitate your exploration of the earth plane.

When you are a goldfish in a bowl, you do not realize that there is a whole other world outside the bowl. It may seem that the world is bowl-shaped, and all you can do is swim in circles. When you look through the glass of the bowl, you see glimpses of something more, but you will never know that air exists. In a way, you are like that fish, and my task is to explain what air is about. Realize that you yourself are in a bowl too, and that the rules that govern time and space in your bowl of time and space are not all there is.

To understand this better, try to imagine what the end of space is like. Trying to figure that out will drive you crazy because figuring that out is way beyond your mental capabilities.

Your mind cannot grasp the concept of what the end of space is like. If you go out billions of light years into the universe, to the last solar system at the end of the universe, you are still always left with the question: And what lies beyond that?

You can do the same exercise with time, trying to imagine the beginning of time. Always the same questions will arise: What existed before that starting point? What occurred before the Big Bang?

These exercises may have shown you that time and space are not what they seem to be. In reality, there is no beginning of time and no end to space. Your linear perceptions of time and space are illusions created by the set of rules of perception that work upon the earth plane. These rules of perception of time and space result in a simplified picture of what reality is like. These restrictive rules create wonderful opportunities, however, to experience your earth with all its beauty and density in forms.

Sets of restrictive rules exist in all kinds of universes for the purpose of bringing about certain densities that give the soul an opportunity to explore these realities. Your reality has time and space as the main restricting rules, but there are many other possible rules.

As you develop your intuitive energy body, you may get glimpses of what lies beyond these restrictions. This gives the soul the opportunity to learn even more.

EARTH CHANGES

Time is not linear

I will now try to give you a concept of what the time and space dimension is really like. The concept of seeing time as space may help you to get the idea.

You might picture time as a circle around you. You are right in the centre. If you start at one point on the circumference of the circle and follow its line, going further away from your starting point, you soon approach the starting point again. Earlier, I used the concept of spirals rather than circles because when you arrive at the starting point in time again, you will find that it is no longer exactly as it was. In fact, your whole experience has been lifted to a higher level.

You might imagine that you, in the center of the circle, represent your soul. Every point on that circle represents a point in time. You can travel around the circumference of the circle. Or, to make the matter more complicated, you can also travel straight outward from your center-point location, crossing the circumference at a ninety-degree angle.

You might conceive of a life you lead as a point on the circumference of the circle. The point moves mostly outward, and inward to the center of the circle, and at the same time it also moves along the circumference of the circle a bit. You might say that time is spiraling upward and inward simultaneously. After many lifetimes, you complete the circle and start again at a higher level.

I must repeat that this model is a simplification because, in fact, there are many more dimensions involved. Talking about these dimensions will lead you to concepts about probable futures and probable selves, which Seth discusses.[7] For our purposes, however, we will not go into that now.

To make things even a bit more complicated, you might

conceive of time as a sphere, instead of a circle. When you conceive of time as a sphere, you may see that it is not only possible to follow one straight line from one point on a circle and arrive at that same point at some other time. On a sphere, you can follow many lines. I only want to touch upon this at this moment and not go into it any further. My goal is just to give you an expanded impression of the nature of time.

Now you may take a break and enjoy the beauty of Heart Lake, which has the power to touch you with the quality and beauty of the universe.

We had been hiking and we had arrived at Heart Lake, a wonderful small lake above Castle Lake. We enjoyed the beautiful view from Heart Lake. Far below lay Castle Lake and behind that Mount Shasta in all its majestic beauty. After a lovely swim in the lake, we continued our walk upward and Phylos went on with the dictation.

Heart Lake

EARTH CHANGES

Space is a manifestation of consciousness

You have done some experiments about the nature of time with us; now let us consider space. For this experiment, we will consider a manifestation of space: matter.

Although you perceive matter as a three-dimensional manifestation in space, the only thing that really exists is consciousness. In your reality right now, you are walking on solid rocks, but in fact, you are walking on nothing but consciousness. Every form is a concept, a manifestation of consciousness. We will illustrate this with another mental experiment.

When you look at the forms that humans have made, what you see is matter. What you really see is ideas put into form, consciousness put into matter. For example, look at your toilet. What you see is a ceramic bowl with a certain form. Of course this is not a coincidental form. A lot of thought has been put into the design: you have to sit on it, there has to be a way for water to go through it, and so on. Every form that exists—in every place that has been constructed by humans—is the result of a conception by human consciousness.

When you look at plants or animals, you also see a manifestation of a plan of consciousness. This plan is put into the seeds and into the DNA.

Also seemingly random forms like rocks, mountains, and the whole mineral kingdom all have a plan and are, in fact, all manifestations of consciousness.

Matter is condensed consciousness

There is another important aspect to this. You might think that, although matter is a manifestation of consciousness, matter is not the same thing that consciousness is. However, when you go to smaller and smaller levels, you will find that matter at its most miniscule level consists of waves of energy. This energy is, in fact, consciousness.

In order to maintain its form, matter must be solid, which means that the consciousness has to stay condensed. This implies that every form has condensed consciousness within itself. A rock, in a way, is conscious of itself.

As you can see, time and space are manifestations of consciousness with limitations imposed upon them in order to create an environment which gives the soul opportunities to explore and to expand its consciousness in the most beautiful ways.

We had stopped on a plateau and now stood on some rocks from which we had a stunning view of Castle Lake and Mount Shasta. Going higher would have been difficult. Phylos suggested that we sit here for a while because it was a power spot in which he wanted to do some work with Froukje to further open her clairvoyant sight.

Welcome, this is Phylos.

I ask you to close your eyes. As we announced yesterday, we will use Froukje's powers of vision today in order to lift some of the veils between the dimensions.

***

P: Both of you may realize that you are at a very sacred spot here. So Froukje, as you connect with the energy of this very holy spot, you may describe the impressions you are getting.

F: I see a Native American looking out at the view from this place.

EARTH CHANGES

P: What does he or she see?

F: Now I see Native Americans falling down off this rock.

P: Describe the scene some more.

F: I see them jumping. They are not afraid, because they know their death will not be the end of their consciousness.

P: Do you see more of this place?

F: I can see some of the lives of those Native Americans before they ended this way.

P: So what do you see?

F: I see the first Native American looking over the lake, enjoying the beautiful view. And I see some kind of ceremony performed with drums and dancing.

P: Continue describing the images. Focus your attention downward into the ground here.

F: There is a kind of hole in the ground, very deep inside the earth.

P: Can you elaborate on this a bit more?

F: There is some kind of a room with someone lying on a table, and there is a tunnel.

P: Who is on the table? What is happening there? You have very good information here because there is a lot going on in a slightly different dimension underneath this place. Look at the walls of the room, maybe the floor, the ceiling.

F: I see golden walls in a rounded shape.

P: Look around and keep describing what you see.

F: I see there is an opening in the ceiling, a tunnel going up inside it. There is light coming through the opening.

P: Right.

F: The person who is lying on the table has his head under this light.

P: What is the purpose of this?

F: This person looks like a being of light.

P: Can you describe this being?

F: It has the shape of a human being but it is made of light. Now I think maybe it's a Native American.

P: What is the person doing there on the table?

F: I don't know. Maybe he is in pain.

P: Is he in pain? You might try to go into that person to find out what he is doing there and who he is.

F: Maybe he is a guard to the other dimensions. I guess he is a kind of gatekeeper. I don't think this person is very happy.

P: Is it a person or a being of light?

F: He is something in between.

P: Do you have any idea why he is not happy?

F: Maybe he doesn't know he is free.

P: Good. If you like we could give some illumination here. What you saw is the Room of Transition between the dimensions of the earth reality and a reality underneath. In this room, the person you saw was a blend of the guard of this room and a person who has entered it. You got the impression of unhappiness because the person who entered knew he was not allowed there. You are in a special place here. These rooms are situated on the outer points of Mount Shasta, and you spotted this one correctly. You did very well.

I would like to thank both of you very much for your work today. Perhaps you can complete this experience by both sending a bit of light to this place of holiness. Unfortunately it is also a place of despair, because Native Americans were killed at this spot.

We say good-bye to you for now with all our love and light.

9.
Beings of Light
McCloud Falls

Today we wanted to visit Medicine Lake, a lake about an hour's drive from Mount Shasta. The Native Americans consider the lake very sacred. It is well known for its healing powers.

Somehow we did not get there. We had many delays, and when we finally arrived in the vicinity of the lake we could not get oriented. After driving back and forth on the main road for a while, both of us in a bad mood, we decided to go back. On our way back, we stopped for a walk at McCloud Falls. As soon as we got there, we felt happy. A very friendly camp host from the campground at the beginning of the trail helped us find our way. We had a beautiful time at these spectacular falls.

Welcome, this is Phylos.

Today you had a lesson in developing your intuitive energy body by means of learning to follow your intuition. Even though you wanted to go to Medicine Lake, this morning and even last night a lot of signs pointed against going there.

First and most meaningful of all, Jeroen woke up at about three o'clock in the morning and his first thought was, Don't go to Medicine Lake. He did not take this thought seriously though because he assumed it came from his personality, and he did not want to spoil the day for Froukje. So he ignored it.

Then there were some signs when you prepared to leave. First, you did not take the time to meditate. When you first felt a bit stressed, you decided it would be easier to meditate when you arrived at Medicine Lake. This was your second opportunity to recognize that you were not to go there. Do not blame yourselves for ignoring these signs. We would not have been able to teach you this lesson in following your intuition if you had not missed them.

Getting ready to leave took you more time than you wanted it to. You had to make a telephone call to Holland after which you felt emotional. Also, Jeroen forgot his shorts so you had to go back to get them. Right from the start, there was a lot of delay.

Then after your long one and one-half hour drive, you never made it to Medicine Lake. On a rational level, you did not make a mistake about the route at all. You just could not believe the signs were right! Therefore you went up and down a few times. That took you another hour.

I must say, I am glad that you finally decided that some guidance might help! Now I can explain this phenomenon: you just did not follow your intuition or the signs of the universe which told you that you should not go there today.

Why today was not a good day to go there is not important for our lesson. Let me say this about it. Yesterday it seemed right to go there. Today the energies have shifted. If you had persisted in going to that lake, you might have had a bad time.

What is important, too, is that now you are walking here by the waterfall, feeling happy, harmonious, and joyful. This was not how you felt this morning. You were both in a bad mood, and from time to time you both felt annoyed. You are used to saying, Well, we will get over it, it is just a bad mood.

What I want to point out is that when you are in a bad mood something is the matter and you should not ignore this.

The universe is coordinated by a higher plan

You may think that things just happen by coincidence, but as you have seen, the universe is guiding you. How is this possible?

As you discovered during our last lesson, everything is a manifestation of consciousness. However, because your capacity to perceive in this world is limited, you underestimate the enormous possibilities of your consciousness. When you realize that every rock and every cell has its own consciousness, you also realize that everything is much more coordinated than you may have previously thought.

You may have a scientific mind and ask, How could all these millions or trillions of molecules possibly behave in an orderly way? Everything must be coincidence.

I tell you it is not. The Higher Will coordinates and guides all.

You are conscious of many more things simultaneously than you normally realize. When you walk, you are conscious of your position on the earth and of what you are saying at the same time. While talking, you can think about other things and also look around. At the same time, you may be aware of all the energies and entities around you although you do not notice them very often with your normal consciousness. Your own being is much more coordinated than you are usually aware of.

All manifestations of consciousness are coordinated at a higher level according to a higher plan.

You may call this the Higher Will. When you look around and see your world, you see a lot of order as well as a lot of seeming chaos. When you look at a specific tree, it may appear different from all other trees, and yet two trees of the same species are much alike. You may think that a plant or tree has a random form, but it does not. Even forms like mountains or a coastline have a plan that is not coincidental at all. Now that you have fractal mathematics and are able to see images of fractals on your computer, your science is getting better at understanding this.[8] These mathematically produced images can look a lot like apparently random forms of coastlines.

Everything works according to a higher plan, and yet at the same time you have freedom. You might say your reality is constructed in a way that gives you limited freedom. Underlying that reality is a plan which defines the boundaries of your freedom. Within that plan, you have a lot of freedom. You have many choices about which paths to follow.

A great deal of guidance is available from the higher realms. There are many higher forms of consciousness in the universe. Mostly, people do not realize this because their conscious attention is absorbed by their daily perception of earth reality. This ordinary perception, however, is only a very limited part of what is possible for you when you move beyond the boundaries created by the restrictive rules that operate on your earth reality. Your true consciousness does not have these boundaries and is totally free.

Your intuition connects you with higher consciousness and with beings of light

You are already perfectly capable of making contact with higher consciousness. You have done this many times already, not with your conscious mind, however, but with your intuition. You use your intuition much more often than you realize. Even the most rational scientists use their intuition a lot.

When you learn to use your intuition consciously for the purpose of connecting with higher consciousness, you may perceive higher beings. They will often look a bit like humans, as we explained earlier. You may also see energies, colors, mathematical forms, or maybe animal forms.

When you contact a higher being, this being reaches out into your dimension with part of its consciousness. Although you do not have the senses to perceive in these other dimensions, your perceptual system makes up an image of this being that more or less fits into your normal world.

You will always create familiar forms even if what comes to you is far from familiar. Your perception works this way. You will always perceive forms that are a bit familiar within your own reality and that are based on your senses and expectations.

However, there is usually a sense that, although the form looks familiar, something out of the ordinary is going on.

What you are mostly able to perceive of the beings that you meet in other dimensions is their auras. Often you mistake these auras for wings since you tend to perceive things that are in accordance with what you know. In paintings, angels or beings from fairy tales are often portrayed as having wings or as wearing special clothing such as long, silky robes.

Do not cling too much to the specific forms you perceive. These are only a way for your perceptual mechanisms to make sense of what you see. It is fine if you see a fairy queen with wings, but do not take the image too literally.

Beings of higher consciousness are guiding you

An important difference between you and beings of higher consciousness is that they are in closer and more direct contact with love, creativity, and intent than you are. They love to help you find your higher path and strengthen your contact with your own love, creativity, and intent.

As it is difficult for you to perceive these beings, they have to find special ways to connect with you. You cannot perceive them in a normal way. They have to find special ways to catch your attention. That is why a lot of guidance works through signs. These signs may seem to come from animals or from nature. They may also take the form of sudden emotions or a particular mood you are experiencing. Guidance may also come while you are dreaming, for your consciousness is most receptive at that time.

If you are willing to strive for higher consciousness, it is of utmost importance to be open to these signs. The more open you are to them, the more easily you will recognize them as signs. However, not all signs are messages from your guides. A bird flying upward may be just a bird flying upward at that moment and have no involvement with you at all. However, it may also be a sign from a guide or another high being to help you open to a perspective you might otherwise have missed. As you practice following your intuition, you will learn which signs are messages from the guides and which are not.

There are different kinds of light beings

Now we will talk about what kinds of beings there are. I will not go into the beings of your world because you have other books in your reality which describe them. I will talk about the beings of light.

EARTH CHANGES

There are light beings of higher and lower consciousness. For example, what you call ghosts are beings of about the same level of consciousness as yours. Actually, they are for the most part humans who have died but still have a strong intent to be on the earth plane. These beings are generally confused. They do not know that they are dead.

Sometimes higher beings are mistaken for ghosts. If someone is very afraid of ghosts and has an encounter with an angel, he may perceive it as a threatening ghost or even as a monster.

That brings me to the topic of monsters. Those species do not exist. At least they do not exist with the bad intentions you put on them. When you perceive a monster, mostly you perceive an entity of light mixed with your own fear. If you have a lot of anxiety, you may see monsters or even devils, and they may even seem to behave just like you believe they should behave.

Then there are extraterrestrial beings. These beings are from other lines of soul development. They do not live on the stars and planets of your reality, but in different dimensions. Because of that, you will not perceive many of them. Some extraterrestrial beings have the capacity to go through the doorways between dimensions, somewhat like angels and other light beings have.

Some extraterrestrials have the ability to create forms that may appear in your reality. When this happens, you may perceive UFOs or extraterrestrial beings. People can find pieces of crashed UFOs, but these pieces are not from machines that fly. The pieces are manifestations of the intersection of your dimension and of the extraterrestrials' dimensions. Extraterrestrial beings may be at about the same level of development of consciousness as you are. However, they may also be more or less evolved.

Then there are beings like me about whom I have been speaking implicitly: guides, angels, masters, and higher beings of light like the great masters. We are all beings of the higher light. Our consciousness is developed to a high level.

At the source of all this is God, which has an enormous consciousness of its own and is the source of all consciousness. At the same time, this consciousness is present in all other forms of consciousness from the simplest stone to the highest evolved Being of Light.

This is the end of this chapter. For now, we say good-bye to you with all our love and light.

10.
Meditation: Deepening Connections
McCloud Falls

Welcome, this is Phylos.

1. Imagine that you are sitting in a power spot near a river.

You can hear the water flowing into a valley. Feel your connection with the earth and feel the energy I am sending you through these words. You may connect with the energy of the Native Americans who once dwelled in these places, their sacred places. They are sacred still. Although no Native Americans are present anymore, their consciousness is still here.

2. While you take some deep breaths, open your energy by imagining that you are breathing in the energy of the universe. Open yourself to the beautiful energy, love, and wisdom of the Higher Will. It may feel as if you are drinking in light, absorbing it with all your cells and with your whole body. Enjoy the clear, soft, soothing light. Feel your connection to the earth and to the universe.

3. Imagine that birds are flying around above you, and watch them until one particular bird draws your attention. Follow its movements as it circles in the sky. Observe its flight pattern; see if you can discover what message the bird is sending you. Use your intuition to pick up the message, which

may or may not make sense to you. It matters not whether your personality understands it consciously. At unconscious levels of your personality and at the level of your soul, you understand the meaning of this pattern.

4. After a while, release the picture of this bird and let come into your mind a picture of a normal bird that is just flying without relaying any message. Maybe it is circling in the sky too. In what way does it move differently than the first bird moved? See or feel the differences. They may be very subtle.

5. Now return to your own energy and move into the center of your being. From this point, observe the patterns of your physical energy. Also observe your etheric body with its lines of light just a few inches beyond your physical body. Next observe your emotional and mental auras even further away from your body.

6. Two angels appear in front of you, one on the left and one on the right. Sense or see their presence. You may see them as forms, colors, or just energy. Or you may only feel their presence. They may resemble pictures you have in your mind of what angels look like. Or they may look very different.

Feel their love and support for you as they hold you in their awareness now. Maybe you can sense their energy coming into your aura, softening it, and weaving patterns of love and light into it. They are working with your energy so that you can connect with the higher beings more easily. Just enjoy this process as long as you like.

7. After you have absorbed enough of their love and energy, thank the angels. Say good-bye to them and return to your own energy. Become aware of your physical form. When you are ready, come back softly, gently, and easily.

11.
The Chosen Ones and Ascension
Panther Meadows—Grey Butte Trail

Welcome, this is Phylos.

We will start our talk after you reconnect with the power stones of Courage and Overview. First, we will pause here for a little while. The Rock of Overview is a very good one to sit on while meditating.

During our last visit to Mount Shasta, Phylos drew our attention to some rocks with special qualities. He said that the rock beside us held the energetic quality of Overview. Another rock nearby held the energetic quality of Courage. Small pieces of these rocks could be used to make elixirs.

Today's chapter is about the chosen ones and ascension.

Who are the chosen ones? They are the ones who are taking a leading role in exploring the expansion of consciousness. You who are reading this are the chosen ones. Before you feel flattered or resistant to this suggestion, I must add that you were chosen by yourself, by your own soul.

Religious texts are interpreted differently in different periods of time

People interpret religious texts differently in different

periods of time. In the world of religion there are misconceptions about this fact, and these misconceptions have far-reaching consequences. People in certain religious groups may think of themselves as the chosen ones. They assume they were chosen by some God-entity and will therefore also be granted special privileges. For example, they may assume they will go to heaven.

In the past, great masters taught a great deal through human channels, and the teachings were often written down. Since human beings cannot easily comprehend the true nature of reality, we use simplified concepts to teach, always adapting our information to the level of consciousness of the specific period of time and culture. We are doing this also with the text you are receiving now.

Some religious texts are written to communicate symbolically and are not meant to be taken as literally as many people take them. For example, some groups view what is called Armageddon as the destruction of the world. In reality Armageddon refers to the shift in consciousness that has already begun and that will continue into the future. Also some groups interpret the concept of "being saved" very literally rather than symbolically as was intended.

Old ways of thinking will not be destroyed, but after this shift in consciousness they will be less important than they were. In a hundred years, people will view some of today's commonly-accepted ideas as simplistic lines of thought, just as people today view some ideas of a hundred years ago as simplistic.

Not all lines of thought that exist today are simplistic, however. Some past civilizations were ahead of their time in that their consciousness was quite expanded. The same is true of some present day civilizations. Consider some Native

American tribes as well as other tribes around the world. Some of their perceptions of reality have been truth for ages and will continue to be truth in the future. As humanity goes through this phase of developing its intuitive energy body, people can learn much from these tribes.

The earth and your consciousness cannot be destroyed

Some people think that Armageddon refers to the destruction of the world. Because humans have free will, they could destroy parts of the world. But the larger plan for the world does not include complete destruction. Many people, especially the chosen ones, are working hard to prevent complete destruction.

Destruction is not quite the correct word. Since it is impossible for humans to destroy the earth completely, do not fear the destruction of the earth: humans simply could not make that happen. The earth is a vast, conscious being. Even if your fear that the earth will be destroyed by nuclear weapons, is realized, the destruction would just end another cycle or spiral in the life of the planet. After some time, maybe after thousands of ages, new life forms and civilizations would emerge. Since consciousness is always seeking new forms, new forms would continue to emerge on the earth plane.

Those who fear the destruction of the earth actually fear their own death. Only physical forms can be destroyed; consciousness cannot. When you realize that neither the earth nor your consciousness can be destroyed, you no longer have a reason to fear the destruction of the earth. What you once thought of as destruction you can now understand as a process of changing form.

Of course, the destruction of the earth's life forms would result in a great loss of beauty and of all the effort and creativity that the earth has put into them. But the earth will restore itself in other ways. Only the forms will disappear. Consciousness will go on forever creating new forms.

You need not worry about your environment. Because of the love you have for the earth's beauty and for the forms that have been created on the earth, you may feel sad about the present state of the earth. This sadness may cause you to want to preserve the earth. But do not worry about its destruction. The earth will always be and so will you. When humans realize that their consciousness cannot be destroyed, their feelings of love and responsibility for the earth will grow. As you humans develop your intuitive energy body, you will begin to know this consciously.

This knowledge will impact how you handle nature and your environment.

If you want the earth and the expressions of consciousness that are on it to continue to be there for some time, you will have to shift into your intuitive energy body. If you make this shift, the present forms may continue to exist and to develop beautifully and harmoniously for many ages.

As you develop your intuitive energy body, you develop your consciousness, especially your love, creativity and intent. You can precipitate this development by treating everything in the world around you with love and respect.

When you treat your environment with love and respect, the earth forms and the earth consciousness will develop, and your consciousness will develop further. Many so-called primitive tribes have been doing this for ages.

EARTH CHANGES

Fear and anger attract disasters; love and respect prevent them

When your actions are motivated by your fears about destruction, you do not prevent catastrophes. In fact, emotions like fear and anger attract catastrophes rather than prevent them. For example, people who fear that they will not have enough, or who get angry about the way other people think and live, may create wars.

People who feel anger are, at a deeper level, also feeling fear—mainly fear of losing their possessions or their life as a result of the deeds of others. When humanity realizes that consciousness is all there is and that consciousness cannot be destroyed, fear and anger will disappear.

Acting out of fear and anger is not the way to prevent the destruction of the earth. However, present mass thinking assumes it is. For example, many environmentalist groups try to use fear to motivate you to contribute money to their cause: they want you to believe that, if you do not give money, the rain forests and the ozone layer will disappear, more people will die of cancer, and so on. What these fear-based environmentalist groups are doing is not the way to prevent catastrophes.

When you first read this, you might not fully appreciate what we are saying. But imagine that your actions and those of every other person on the earth were respectful of nature. Exploitation of the earth's resources would stop, happiness would increase, and materialism would diminish significantly. If you lived in harmony with nature, perfect happiness would be the result. You do not need ever-greater varieties of food, or more meat, and so on. You only need some basics to stay alive and to be happy.

You do not have to go back to nature completely and

discard cars and television and all the things that humanity has developed. As you develop your intuitive energy body, those material things will develop in ways that are in harmony with nature. Your scientists cannot yet grasp the material forms that will develop. For example, parts of UFOs that were found on the earth are puzzling scientists who are unable to reproduce them. In fact, these parts consist of a combination of material forms and intuitive thought forms.

When you live in a harmonious and respectful way with your environment, your need for more and more of everything will disappear. What will evolve instead is your need for perfect, loving, creative, and high forms.

Your soul calls you to take a leading role

Now I will return to the subject of the chosen ones. In this lifetime, you have been chosen by your soul to be at the forefront of the development of consciousness on the earth. Unfortunately, this may trigger some personality issues, but I cannot deny this truth.

Why are you doing this while others are not? In this lifetime you are on a path chosen by your soul to help you achieve a high level of development. Perhaps in another lifetime, or as another self in this lifetime, your soul has chosen a different path. Perhaps in another life, you are destroying the earth and making a lot of money without considering others or the environment.

However, in this lifetime and in this form you have chosen a higher path of soul development. All development of your soul, higher and lower, serves to expand its consciousness as a whole and with that the consciousness of the Oneness. When you expand your consciousness, you send light out into the planet's gridwork of light, making light more accessible to all human beings, enabling them to expand their consciousness as well. The more you live from the perspective of your soul, the higher and more expanded your consciousness will be. The second part of this book will discuss how to live as a soul on the earth.

We have not spoken explicitly about ascension here, but I will do so briefly now. At some point in your development, you may reach such high levels that you become an ascended master yourself. This is possible for every soul because every conscious form, by its very nature, strives to express itself in higher forms. One of these higher forms is that of ascension. Ascended beings are free to choose the forms in which they will or will not appear on the earth.

Most likely, you will not become an ascended master in one lifetime. But it is possible that you could become enlightened in one lifetime. When you are enlightened, you have attained complete clarity about who you really are and what your purpose in that lifetime is. This clarity is not a rational understanding but a direct inner knowledge. When you reach enlightenment, you are in close contact with higher love, creativity, and intent. Even if you have developed these qualities of enlightenment, however, you have still not attained the ascended masters' level of consciousness and freedom.

***

P: Froukje, please restate the question you asked during the break.

F: I feel frustrated that that we are, in this lifetime, following a higher path (about which I am, in fact, a little proud) while at the same time, in another lifetime or parallel reality, we may be doing just the opposite.

P: Some of the material we are teaching may be frustrating to your personality and you may find yourself asking, "What is the sense of this—in this life, I am doing things that I am proud of, while in another life I am being destructive?"

Here again, I must emphasize that consciousness is always striving toward a higher level.

On a personality level, you may be proud of living well. You are also living a simultaneous life in which you are doing things you disapprove of from your current perspective. That does not change the fact that you are living well now. You may realize that in your simultaneous life you are developing qualities that make it possible to bring your current life to a higher level as well.

Since time and space are only concepts of earth plane reality, you might say that other lifetimes are going on at the same moment.

Perhaps in another life, you just destroyed a beautiful environment by digging an oil well and letting the oil flow over your land and that of your neighbors. Maybe that experience in that life helps you discover something about beauty and respect for nature. This may enhance your sense of beauty and your respect for nature in your current life. Actually, there should not be any frustration at all. Being "bad" is also a way of learning.

Does this answer your question?

F: Yes. I have another question. Why do our souls choose for us to live and grow the way we do while other souls make different choices?

P: Every soul strives toward its own development. The older the soul, the more interest it has in developing its consciousness in the manner that you are developing yours.

Talking about older and younger souls is difficult since there is no time in our dimensions.

EARTH CHANGES

Again, I will use the concept of spiraling to illustrate my point. You can visualize a time spiral as a three-dimensional form. On such a spiral, you can be on higher and lower levels. In reality, you cannot speak of older and younger souls. Speaking about the levels of soul development would be more accurate. Nevertheless, when you translate this into earth terms by putting a time perspective on it, you might say that in this life your soul is older than some other souls.

Souls of the same "age" have a tendency to connect with each other. That is why, for example, many people in your country may be attracted to meditation, whereas people in another country may not have much interest in meditation. Different groups of people may have different lines of soul development. Soul connections also occur in dimensions other than your three-dimensional world. Does this answer your question?

F: Yes.

P: Then we will end this chapter now. We say good-bye to you for now with all our love and light.

12.
Words of Good-bye

Mount Shasta, higher slopes

As our stay at Mount Shasta came to a close, the masters invited us to hike on the higher slopes of the mountain around sunset. They guided us to a flat, round spot where they wanted to speak some words of good-bye. From this place, the orange sunlight shining on the mountain was a most stunning sight.

Welcome, this is Phylos.

Look at the sheer beauty of the mountain at this time of the day!

We, the ascended masters, are glad that you have come here for our words of good-bye. We do hope it will not be good-bye forever. We have lots more to teach and we invite you to come you back at another time.

There are doorways between dimensions and you can move through them

As you can feel, the energy is very high here right now.

Depending on what time you leave, you may or may not see the lights that come from within the mountain. They are visible at night for people who are ready to see them. Do not be afraid of these lights, these are just energy reflections of the inner mountain at the doorway between the dimensions.

Yesterday on the summit of Grey Butte, we met Neil and his wonderful little dog, Rosy. They were staying at the highest parking lot on Mount Shasta. He told us that every night he saw soft lights emerge in a rhythmical pattern from a place a bit higher on the mountain. This went on for hours. Since we left Mount Shasta before dark, we did not see the lights ourselves.

As you have learned in the meditations, when you draw your attention into the very core of your being, you find a small point of light. When you pass through it with your awareness, you come into the enormous space of the soul plane. There are a few more of these points. You move through the doorways to other dimensions by spiraling inward. The smaller the points you enter, the larger the spaces that open for you. A doorway is often a bright point of light which becomes brighter as you approach it. When you go through it, you enter a vast space.

We used the point of light in the core of your being to find the vastness of the soul plane. There are also some other points of light. The mental energy body, the emotional energy body, and the intuitive energy body each have one. When you move through these points, you enter different spaces.

The emotional transition point brings you into the sea of love-energy. The mental transition point brings you to the vast plane of higher knowledge. The transition point of the intuitive energy body, which is really a transition point behind a transition point, brings you to the angelic spheres of higher will, love, and creativity.

There are more transition points. While developing your psychic ability, you may pass through the doorway of your third eye. Some other time we will reveal more about these transition points. Experiencing them is more important than receiving information about them, so we will continue with our meditations and teach more about these points at another time.

The lessons we have taught you during these past days have been about some basic issues of consciousness and the phase in which humanity now exists. We began with these topics so that you would have some good, basic information to build upon. We hope the meditations gave you an experiential base for understanding these energies.

We will elaborate on these topics later. For now, we wish to address in a practical way the topic of how to live well on the earth plane. Our subsequent lessons will discuss how to handle your emotions and thoughts, and how to develop your intuitive energy body.

We the ascended masters of Mount Shasta are assembling around you right now. We suggest that you go to that point over there on the ridge and stop there to receive our words of good-bye. From there you may also see or sense the light on the mountain that your friend saw.

We did as Phylos asked and climbed the ridge, where we found a flat, round, open space in between the rocks. We stopped here and Phylos resumed his words.

Good. For this occasion, we ask you to stand in the middle of this circle and look around. Feel the energy of the mountain and the moon. Face the mountain, and now close your eyes.

We, the ascended masters of Mount Shasta, say good-bye to you with open hearts.

We acknowledge you for your willingness to bring these

materials through to humanity. We are working with you and some others like you who are committed and willing to open to our energies.

We welcome you back to this mountain at another time of your choosing. We will be glad to meet with you again. We feel a deep love for you and for the people who read our material.

We want to encourage all of you who have the courage to find your higher path to listen to the whispers of your soul, and to be flexible and open to new ideas. In addition, we encourage you to be open to ways of living that are not always in alignment with the main stream of humanity, and, in fact, sometimes seem to be going against that stream.

As we say good-bye now, feel the energy of the mountain and of this holy circle in which you now stand. Open yourself again to receive our transmissions to you—and beyond you to the readers of this material.

With this, we conclude our September teachings on Mount Shasta. We say good-bye with all our love and light.

PART 2
Living Well

13.
Soul Contact
Mount Shasta

In March, six months after the masters spoke their words of goodbye, we returned to Mount Shasta. The mountain looked magnificent, most of it still covered with lots of snow. We had pitched our tent at a campground in the valley. Many of the wonderful hikes we had last summer were not possible during this season. However, we enjoyed walking in the snow.

Welcome, this is Phylos announcing that a big energy shift for humanity is coming soon.

We welcome you back. We have great love for you and for all who are helping humanity to prepare for this shift. During the next days we will talk about how to live well, which means how to live in accord with your soul's purpose.

Your physical body needs food and drink, your emotional body needs love and harmony, your mental body needs to have higher thoughts in order to evolve. Your intuitive energy body needs inspiration from the soul. We could say it needs food from the soul.

The upcoming chapters discuss how you can achieve clearer and more direct soul contact so that you can feed and develop your intuitive energy body.

This chapter describes the conditions of earth life, and

how these conditions make it difficult for your soul to stay in touch with you.

As we said before, the earth is a world of divisions. It has a certain density that gives the soul many opportunities to learn. In order to survive, you have to adapt to the conditions of the earth. Your first step is to incarnate on the earth, and in order to do this you must become denser. This means that your soul must materialize a physical body.

Your soul materializes your physical body in steps in which the energies become progressively denser. During this process, your soul uses transition points at which energies from the soul combine and bundle. Close to your physical body, your soul spreads its energy out again to form your physical body and your energy bodies.

A small part of your soul extends into the earth dimension, but most of it exists in other dimensions. The transition points and focusing lines cross dimensions.

Your soul interacts with you continuously

We will now talk a bit more about the energy bodies: the *physical*, the *etheric*, the *emotional*, the *mental*, and the *intuitive*, which is now developing.

The dimension closest to your physical body is the etheric. Your physical body is kept alive and fed by your soul through the etheric body. It is a kind of a layer between your soul reality and the reality of the earth plane.

Next comes your emotional body. Your emotions also exist in dimensions other than your earth plane dimensions.

Although people take their emotions for granted, they are unable to picture their emotions in a three-dimensional reality. It is not possible to photograph, paint, or sculpt emotions. In fact, it is a miracle that nobody ever wonders about where, in what dimensions, emotions actually exist. While everyone agrees that they are present, nobody knows where they are. Emotions are actually located in another dimension, just as the etheric body is. Yet everyone can perceive them clearly. This is one of the reasons the soul often communicates with the personality through the emotions. This is especially the case with people who have not yet developed more direct ways of soul contact.

The emotions function to communicate with the soul. What you call intuition is, in fact, a message from the soul given to you through your emotions. Sometimes you may experience a sudden feeling or emotion that does not seem appropriate to the earthly conditions of that moment. You may, indeed, recognize this as a message from your soul. These experiences are very common. You have probably heard people talk about having a good or a bad feeling about something. On a subconscious level, people usually know more about this interaction with their soul than their conscious mind realizes.

Next comes the mental body. The mental body is also located in another dimension and sends its energy waves into the physical dimension.

Emotions and thoughts have a physical manifestation as well. When an emotion or a thought comes up, chemical reactions occur in the physical body. These chemical reactions are the physical manifestations of the energy transitions between the dimensions. You can detect these energy transitions with your normal senses. Some scientists incorrectly assume the reverse and believe that emotions and thoughts are the *result* of chemical processes. If you believe this, you will never be able to understand why these chemical reactions occur.

The intuitive energy body is an energy body that is close

to the soul and also to earth reality. The intuitive energy body has great potential for direct communication with your soul and with other beings in the higher multidimensional realms of reality. Humans can now develop this energy body more fully than they could in the past.

You may be confused about the word intuition. The intuitive energy body does not facilitate communication between the soul and the personality by means of feelings, as the emotional energy body does. The intuitive energy body facilitates communication between the soul and the personality by way of a direct knowing which comes from the higher realms, not from your mental energy body. For example, you receive the information we are giving you right now with your mind, but you know what is useful to you because your intuition has a direct knowing of that.

Thoughts come from many different levels

Your thoughts consist of a mixture of knowledge which you have received from different levels. First, is the knowledge that is stored in your personality and sent out to the mental energy body which reflects it back as thoughts. These thoughts you might, at least partially, claim as your own.

Second, are patterns of thought you have in common with all people of your species. These thoughts come from what we call humanity's "common" mental energy body. Your mental energy body is connected to this much larger mental energy field. The common mental energy body contains the mass thought forms of your time in addition to the common knowledge which a human being requires to stay alive.

Third, are thoughts that are that are transmissions from the higher realms. These may come from your soul or even from beyond your soul as transmissions of the plan of humanity and the world.

The mental energy body is a mixture of all of these energies. Refining your inner senses helps you recognize which thoughts come from where. This may take quite a lot of training.

Many of the ideas you get are not your own but come from outside. People often think that many of the behaviors and thoughts you share with other people are stored in your genes. But this is not so. These thoughts and behaviors are transmitted to you from humanity's common mental energy body. Your genes are a storage place for some information, but if you do not have a connection to the mental energy body and the higher realms, you cannot activate the information in your genes.

You are able to transcend the conditions of earth

In order to adapt to this denser world, you need equipment in the form of your energy bodies. In order to survive on this physical plane, you have to become denser yourself. This state of affairs exists for a reason, namely to give you beautiful opportunities to learn. These opportunities are much more readily available than you realize. Enlightenment is at your fingertips, but you seldom realize that.

You need not go to the Himalayas or to Mount Shasta to become enlightened. You can do it everywhere. Enlightenment is that state in which you are in direct, open contact with your soul and your higher source, unaffected by all the restrictions and distortions created by the human condition.

Before we go into the subject of how to connect with this direct knowledge and contact your source, we will talk a bit about the conditions of life on the earth that make it so difficult for you to make this connection.

Your senses create an illusion of your world

The main feature of this world is its reality of divisions. It consists of endless contrasts and polarities: dry and wet, black and white, love and hate, and so on. There are always two poles. The only reason you know about one pole is because you know about the other pole. A fish swimming in its bowl does not know that it is in water as long as it does not know about the existence of an outside world with an environment that is not water, but air.

In order to survive in this world of polarities, you need to be able to adapt and habituate to many different conditions. Without adaptation and habituation, you would not survive because you would have to invent and learn about this world anew every moment.

Adaptation is the process of learning to predict the conditions of this world. Predicting the conditions of your environment is necessary for survival. To survive in the earth dimension you need to know, for example, to know what to eat, which animals are dangerous, and that you can walk through air but not through solid rocks.

Habituation is the process of getting used to every condition you encounter in your world. This is an important survival mechanism since it allows you to direct your attention to things other than the condition you just encountered. For example, you may be injured in an accident. After a while your perception of pain will diminish, enabling you to do whatever is necessary to escape from the situation.

Adaptation and habituation work at every level of the personality. You truly get used to this world.

For some, adaptation and habituation may even result in boredom. We find it hard to believe that anyone could get bored in your world since from our perspective everything there is an absolute wonder. Everything you see, smell, taste, or feel is a wonder of the earth plane. However, the mechanisms of adaptation and habituation allow you to become accustomed to wonders, to take them for granted, and even to be bored by them. Right now you are even used to the fact that I am speaking through you!

What is more, on the earth plane you have a highly specialized set of senses with which you can perceive very specific energies. These energies are only a small proportion of all the energies that you may perceive from more expanded levels of consciousness as you become more enlightened. The information coming in through these senses is perceived and interpreted by your inner senses. In order to adapt to the earth conditions, your senses make you believe that what they tell you is what your world is really like.

Your senses may even trick you. If you perceive things that are unfamiliar to your world, your senses will distort these things in such a way that they become coherent with what you are used to perceiving. For example, when you encounter extraterrestrial beings, you will perceive them as humanoid. Sometimes your senses refuse to perceive unfamiliar objects at all.

Enlightenment is at your fingertips

When you break through the illusion created by your senses, you will be able to perceive every possible feature of the here and now in a completely open way. When you are able to perceive in such an open way, you will know the world by way of direct knowing, that is, by using your intuitive energy body instead of your physical senses. In this state of enlightenment, you will perceive the world as energy, "seeing" all energies directly as they are.

In a way, this is the most natural and easy thing to do because in your natural state of being you have an open consciousness. Perception by way of the senses and the mechanisms of adaptation and habituation are only tools needed for living in the denser energies of the earth plane. However, the illusion that is created by your senses and by the processes of habituation and adaptation is so strong that it is very difficult for the personality to break the spell.

So why break this spell? Why become enlightened?

Enlightenment does not imply complete distraction from life on the earth plane. Being enlightened on the earth plane means being on the earth plane with your full consciousness. When you reach this stage, you are connected with and completely open to your soul, without the veils that normally blur this contact during your life on earth.

Normally, because of the illusion created by your senses and by the processes of adaptation and habituation, only a small part of your consciousness is available to you in this world. You have to exert a lot of effort to widen the scope of your consciousness.

When you aim for enlightenment, you aim to be fully conscious of your world and of yourself—the being that you really are. Enlightenment means full contact with your higher source, your soul, and the higher forces of the universe.

Consider the process of eating a meal. You can enjoy every little bit of food at a much deeper level when you open all your senses—your taste, your smell, your vision, and your knowledge about what you are eating. Another example might be listening to classical music. If you are not familiar with it, you may not like it. However, when you open up to it with all of your consciousness, you can have a beautiful experience. When you have more knowledge or consciousness of the music, you may hear or even see the patterns in it and behind it. When you open and expand your consciousness, you generally see and find more patterns in all things about you.

You can break the spell of what your senses tell you

The first guideline to help you break the spell of the illusions is to begin to expand your consciousness by enjoying what your senses are telling you in a more conscious way. As you increase your enjoyment of your sensory experiences, you are truly deepening your consciousness.

For example, when you eat, try to concentrate only on the process of eating and on the taste of the food. Take small bites, chew well, and enjoy every bite of what you eat with your full consciousness. In this way, eating becomes a kind of meditation in taste. You can do the same exercise with hearing, seeing, or smelling.

As you do these exercises, you may quickly notice yourself in a process of habituation. When you eat an apple, the first bite will have a lot of taste, the second a bit less, and so on as you quickly habituate to the taste of the apple.

The second guideline is to stay focused on the taste throughout the whole experience. While you eat an apple, experience its taste as fully as you can with every bite. Meditate on the taste of each bite and, at the same time, on the habituation process. Try to prevent habituation from interfering with the experience of tasting every bite of the apple.

The third guideline is to enjoy the process. When you first

start meditating, it may seem like an exercise. As you get used to the exercise, however, it becomes pure joy. Pure joy is a state of expanded consciousness that can be reached in this way.

In order to be effective, a meditation like this should be done for at least twenty minutes daily. I am choosing the example of a meditation on taste because this meditation is easy to do while eating, something you will be doing anyhow.

When you do this kind of meditation, you expand your consciousness by way of the senses. When you use your senses as fully and openly as possible, with as little habituation as possible, you are opening your consciousness to be free of the senses.

The fourth guideline is to seek the essence of what a particular sense is telling you. If you are looking at the color green or red, which you can see now while walking here, you might try to grasp the energy-essence of these colors.

The fifth guideline is to read and learn about what you are doing at a mental level. This can help you deepen your experience. For example, people who enjoy drinking wine can enhance their taste experience of the wine and the joy they find in drinking it by reading about how it is made. The same principle applies when you are observing birds or plants. Learning and reading about them brings more consciousness into your enjoyment of them. And studying art enhances how colors affect you.

When you deepen your consciousness in such a way, you may notice that you perceive more than you did before and that you feel more enthusiastic about the subject.

It is important that this gaining of knowledge gives you joy. Do not go to a museum if you just think that you should go there for your education. Only go there if you have a joyous feeling about it, when you get a message from your soul telling you that visiting a museum is a good step at this point in your development.

In this chapter, we offered some processes that can be performed daily to achieve enlightenment and deeper contact with your soul. These processes have ordinary reality as their starting point. Later we will give you processes and forms of meditation that are closer to the soul.

This is the end of this chapter. For now, we say good-bye to you with all our love and light.

14.
Playing the Earth Game: The Rules of the Game

Castle Crags—Indian Springs Trail

Castle Crags

Welcome, this is Phylos. We reach out to you. And we reach out to the ancient and holy Lemurian slopes of Castle Crags. This area holds a lot of Native American energy.

Today's chapter will be about playing the earth game and the rules of this game.

Your thoughts are based mainly upon survival mechanisms

As we explained earlier, you must possess certain survival mechanisms to survive on the earth plane. We have already discussed the senses and the mechanisms of adaptation and habituation. Your mind and your thoughts, with which you often identify yourself, are also survival mechanisms. Many of your thoughts have little or nothing to do with the being that you truly are.

In order to play the earth game, you first need to have a good understanding of these mechanisms. Expanding your consciousness will give you a clear understanding of which survival mechanisms you are using. Once you have this understanding, you need to consciously expand beyond these mechanisms. When you do that, you will be living on two levels. The first level is the level of the earth plane. The second level is a higher level on which you will use your intuitive energy body to live your life from a higher perspective, seeing yourself and the world as they really are.

In a way, your mind and your way of thinking are reflections of your survival mechanisms and the fear involved in them. Many of the thoughts you have, for example, about the money you desire, the house you want to live in, or the things you choose to have around you, are based upon deep fear related to survival. Simply put, if an animal is hungry it will start to develop more ways to get food. Many of your belongings today reflect your fear of not having enough and of not being able to survive.

Often people do not realize this fact. A wealthy person will often buy a big house, an expensive car, and so on. These actions are, in fact, based on fear. There is no real beauty in a Ferrari except in its design. However, even a scale model of the Ferrari might do for seeing the beauty of it. Owning the real car is really a symbolic way of saying, Look, I am important, I am rich. Do not try to harm me; I have power.

What I am saying about the Ferrari is also true for a lot of other symbols in your society. I am not saying that you should not have cars or that you should not have beautiful cars. I want you to realize the symbolic meaning of the exaggerated emphasis on material forms. When you go to higher levels of consciousness, you will find that real beauty most often lies in simplicity and efficiency of forms.

The way you think and the way you use language are also based on survival mechanisms. All language is based on contrasts and divisions. Your life too is full of contrasts. Doing contrasts with not doing. A thing contrasts with no-thing.

These contrasts and divisions are illusions of the earth reality. Nevertheless, they make earth life possible. In that sense, you may consider them as survival mechanisms. But on the higher planes, these contrasts and divisions do not exist.

Your thoughts, which are mostly based on language, are mainly a reflection of the way you think your world is constructed. Most of your thoughts, like most of your senses, reinforce your illusions about the world and how it is made.

Words cannot describe your true being

The rationality of your mind is a helpful tool for surviving on the earth plane in that it creates divisions and handles them. However, it is also a handicap to lifting the veils of the earth plane and to truly seeing the earth plane for what it is.

Interestingly enough, your rationality helps you maintain an image of this world as a constant thing, yet you could easily see that earth is not a constant thing. Your rational mind tries to convince you that you behave in an orderly, rational manner. But when you look, for example, at a person sitting behind a desk and you observe his movements, you will see that he makes many movements which do not make any sense at all. He scratches somewhere, moves his fingers, moves his arms—all are meaningless behaviors. The mechanisms of adaptation and habituation cause you to not pay attention to them. You just live your life without questioning why people are making all kinds of irrational and unnecessary movements. The rational mind sees what it wants to see and tends to neglect the evidence that the world is not as rational as it seems to be.

Your rationality, the function of which is to hold up your image of the world, also uses the mechanism of norms. Once you accept a certain worldview you no longer feel a need to question it. A child who is still open to all of the energies and wonders that are present on earth will always ask questions: Why is this? Why is that? Since the answers can never be satisfactory, the adult answers jokingly, That's just the way it is.

If you take anything in your world and start asking Why? about it, you will soon discover that your rationality cannot handle the issue.

"Daddy, why do things fall downward?"

"Well my child, it's because of gravity."

"Well, why is that? What is gravity?"

"Gravity is a force which makes things go down when you drop them."

"Oh, why is that?"

Now Daddy is out of words. Because he feels there is something that has to be explained, he may start to study mathematical formulas about how gravity works. Still this does not solve the basic question about what gravity is.

If you start asking Why is this? or What is this? about any subject, you will soon find yourself at a dead end. Try any subject you like. We suggest you meditate on what a color is like, what a specific taste is like, what an emotion is like, or what a thought is like. It is impossible to answer these questions in a way that the rational mind can understand. Often such questions are considered childish. The fact is, however, that most of norms are created by you humans to maintain your assumption that you have an ongoing identity and an ongoing world.

The rational mind gives the personality a sense of safety by providing it with an illusion of constancy in the world. The concept of linear time is also a creation of the rational mind. The idea that the earth is a material and predictable thing is also such a creation.

Your senses reflect only a small portion of the universe

We have tried to explain that your world as you perceive it is only a reflection of what the universe and you are truly about. There are sets of rules operating on the earth plane that you need to follow to be able to survive and to learn in this realm. You have senses that allow you to do this, but they reflect only a very limited range of all the energies present. They reflect, perhaps, one percent, or maybe one hundredth or one thousandth of a percent, of the energies in the universe, depending on how large the scale and how numerous the dimensions you involve in your perceptions.

Your world is a world of dense energy. In order to survive you have to use dichotomies, divisions, and contrasts. Your world is built of these elements, and this fact is reflected in your thoughts. Also the mechanisms of adaptation and habituation are necessary to be able to make predictions in your world, so you can live with an illusion of constancy.

These conditions are only tools which make living on the earth plane possible. When you can see these tools as merely tools, you may be able to step out of these limited conditions and get in touch with who you really are.

Before we discuss how to step out of these conditions, we will make a few remarks about society. During the last millennium, your society became more of a reflection of these tools and less a reflection of your true being. In a society of divisions, you need things like money, belongings, property, ideas of good and bad, and a justice system. You need all kind of ideas and forms that reflect your "toolkit" world. When you step out of this toolkit system and you no longer identify with the tools but with the consciousness that uses the tools, your expanded consciousness will show you that your society has become much too rigid. You will see that all kinds of boundaries have been created by humans that do not really exist in the universe.

It is as though you are a carpenter who believes the world consists of planks and nails, and you no longer see or know that the wood comes from beautiful trees and the iron from beautiful rocks. If, as a society, you would see the beauty of the trees and the rocks and not just the planks and the nails, you would step out of this system of divisions. If you develop your intuitive energy body, you will find it much easier to evolve toward your true being and destination in the new millennium.

This is the end of this chapter. For now, we say good-bye to you with all our love and light.

15.
Doorways

Castle Crags—Indian Springs

Now we will go on with the next chapter. We will discuss some doorways through which you may pass to expand into your true self and become enlightened.

Until now, we have used your language and your mental forms to prepare you to open your consciousness, and to translate higher knowledge into a form your earthly being understands.

The first doorway is to understand that you and your world are just a very small proportion of what your true self and the world are really about. When you have a rational understanding of this, you may become interested in searching further. For that reason, we call this rational understanding the first doorway. You must pass through this doorway to be able to expand into your true being and become enlightened.

The second doorway is to use the tools we talked about and expand their scope. You can accomplish this with your mental energy body by, for example, continually asking questions and thinking about possible answers—until you are meditating on unsolvable riddles, the way Zen meditators do. And, as we mentioned previously, you can also meditate on essences like taste or color. The more you practice in your daily life, the more consciousness you gain.

The third doorway is to live your life in such a way that it best reflects the purposes of your soul and the being that you really are. You may or may not already be in contact with the being that you really are and receive its guidance. Your goal is to live in accord with your true being and its purposes, and with the purposes of the higher beings of the universe.

The fourth doorway is to develop your inner senses by looking inward. This doorway involves focusing your attention inward in meditation. In meditation you can rediscover how your inner senses work and develop close contact with the being that you really are. You may enter states of consciousness that are beyond words.

Actually, the word *develop* is not quite the correct one since these inner senses are already developed. Most people, however, have forgotten how to use their inner senses because human socialization processes focus so greatly on developing survival mechanisms.

Listen to your inner senses and to the "rumble" in your thoughts

As we said before, enlightenment is at your fingertips. But in a practical sense, enlightenment is not that easy to attain because of your life-long neglect of your inner senses. In your earth being, you have a set of highly-developed inner senses that can connect you with the larger being that you really are and with the powers of the universe. Moment by moment, your whole life long, you are guided by these senses and by the information they pick up from your higher self and from the universe.

The point is that this guidance is so extremely natural for you that you do not even notice it. When you do notice it, your mental toolkit tries to explain it in rational ways. Most of your thoughts are based on your survival mechanisms, but about fifteen percent of your thoughts come from your higher self and soul. Usually you ignore these. They are what you call the "rumble" in your thoughts. Often you dismiss this rumble; you think you are merely being distracted or having daydreams. When you do that, you are already placing a judgment on the thoughts that come from your soul. You are saying that these thoughts are not real thoughts. I tell you that all that rumble and all those distractions are in reality messages from your soul.

Real distortions in your thinking do exist though. For example, if someone harms you even without intending to, you may immediately think about harming that person in return, even if you are not at all an aggressive person. You may feel that your thoughts do not reflect the being that you wish to be, and dismiss them as rumble.

Your rational mind automatically evens up your world by thinking such thoughts because your reality, by its very nature, is always divided. The Divine created your reality by splitting part of itself off from the Oneness. This resulted in your reality of divisions. Every thought you have is the counterpart of a non-thought. A strong force in the universe strives for completion, for the reunification of parts into wholeness or oneness. If an aspect of your thinking seems to be incomplete, your mind will try to complete it, even if the resulting thoughts do not reflect the being that you truly are.

Earlier we gave an example of how your mind evens things up. You might consider this process to be a distortion of your thinking, which is an outcome of the dichotomous way your mind works. Your mind's tendency to even things up is automatic and does not reflect your true being. Only love, creativity, and intent exist at the higher levels of the universe. Punishment and revenge are not part of the universe of abundant love. Therefore, we could say that dichotomous thoughts are distortions.

Since your rational mind is only a survival mechanism and you are in essence a spiritual being, you are able to transcend the dichotomous way your mind works. When you recognize your mind's natural tendency to even things up, you can simply dismiss many thoughts. Actually most of you do this already; you filter out many of these thoughts before they reach your conscious awareness. Unfortunately, many humans just act on their thoughts without first questioning the validity of these thoughts. Such behavior can result in wars. When you fight another human being, you fight yourself since you are, at the highest levels, all one.

Fifteen percent of your thoughts are messages from your soul. Most of you normally neglect them. About half of the rest of your thoughts are about how to even up other thoughts.

The mental part of your intuition is the fifteen percent of your thoughts that are the rumble that comes from your soul. Your intuition often contains great ideas. It also has an emotional component. The ideas and emotional messages from your soul are available to you. You can learn to pay attention to them. We will help you do this in the meditation after this chapter.

Your moment-by-moment perception of the world is guided by impulses and thoughts from your higher self and soul. You hardly notice these thoughts. Your rational mind may try to find reasons for all your actions, including your daily actions, but it will find only circular explanations. It may try to explain why you place your feet the way you do, why you start brushing your teeth on the left side and not the right, and so on. You can understand these matters better if you understand the mechanism of guidance from your higher self, your soul, and the other forces and beings of the universe.

This is the end of this chapter. We say good-bye to you for now with all our love and light.

16.
Meditation: Catching Higher Thoughts
Indian Springs

Welcome, this is Phylos.

1. Begin by taking a few breaths. Breathe in and out. On the exhale, imagine that you are growing larger and that your energy is expanding. On the inhale, feel our energies, and connect with the energies of the sacred place called Indian Springs. In this beautiful place in the mountains, a spring emerges from a moss-covered rock and gives pleasant moisture to the air. With every breath, you become larger, connecting more and more with our energies.

If you have any thoughts, just observe them. Let the thoughts that you would normally consider valid and rational disappear. Just let them flow outward with your expanding energy.

2. Notice that your energy starts to clear up. The clouds in it are disappearing; the sunshine is coming in. Now focus on that process of clearing, and let your attention be drawn into that place of greater light. Observe the thoughts and feelings that come up.

3. Try to catch your thoughts. They may appear in the corner of your eye as soft whispers on the edges of your perception. At first, your thoughts may seem like images or half sentences that you try to grasp. If thoughts about your

daily world interfere, just let those disappear. Keep expanding with every exhalation. You are carried by the energy of this place and by our energies. You may feel or see light, which shines more and more brightly through the clouds of your consciousness.

Maybe at first the thoughts or images you perceive do not make much sense. That is a good sign. Or you may feel that you are not grasping anything at all, that your thoughts are quiet. That is good as well because you have created an opening. Just let this silence be and continue with the process of expanding your energy and sending ordinary thoughts away. As you visualize the opening of light, let your thoughts disappear and dissolve in your ever-expanding energy.

4. Now come back slowly. First, draw your energy back to you. When your energy is back, inhale deeply. Stretch your body and open your eyes. You may feel a deeper quiet, more peace. Now your soul is close to you.

It matters not whether you have seen or heard or thought anything at a conscious level. In this meditation, you have made an opening through which your higher self and soul can guide you.

For now, we say good-bye to you with all our love and light.

17.
Higher Love, Creativity, and Intent
Parking lot on Mount Shasta

Welcome, this is Phylos. This chapter is about higher love, creativity, and intent. As your soul travels on the earth plane, you can learn a lot by following the principles of living well. Different masters have explained how to live well, and their advice has always been much the same. Nevertheless, we will give it to you in our own words.

Learn to tune in to your soul

On the earth plane, the best way for you to grow is by living in close contact with your soul and the higher forces of the universe.

To accomplish this, you first need to spend time connecting with your soul and the higher forces of the universe and to become more aware of your contact with All There Is. At this time, humanity is very interested in manipulating matter. Humanity is also interested in manipulating the mental, as is reflected in many people's need for discussion. Although exploring this beautiful planet and its possibilities in mental ways is not wrong, you can learn a great deal more when you turn your attention inward and contact your soul. If you meditate and tune in to that fifteen percent of your thoughts that consists of messages from your soul, you will receive a lot of guidance about how to handle your life on the earth.

We do not want you to retreat from earth life completely and only draw your attention inside, but we do advise that you take time daily to tune in to the messages from your soul and from the higher realms. If you do, you will learn how to create a higher quality daily life. As you bring more love, creativity, and intent into your daily life, the quality of your life will improve.

Daily love and higher love

First, we will speak of the difference between what we call *daily love* and *higher love*. Daily love is the kind of love you experience when you fall in love with someone and are very excited about it. Daily love may or may not last long. If, however, your feeling of falling in love comes from your soul as it guides you toward a soul mate, you are experiencing a higher form of love. When people stay with each other for long periods and tune inward, daily love may become higher love. Higher love is love that is fed by the soul. You might also say that higher love is deep compassion or a deeply felt sense of joy. In higher love, aspects like gratitude, peace, and feelings of harmony with nature are also involved.

Higher love may also be referred to as *soul love* because when you are in contact with your soul you can easily connect with these higher qualities.

Higher love between people is unconditional. In the more earthly states of love, love is conditioned by the gains and losses it may cause your personality to experience. You may find this hard to believe while you are falling in love;

during that process you do not easily see that gains and losses are involved. However, when you consider a past episode of falling in love, you may recognize that you were influenced by personality gains and losses. For example, you may have felt more worthwhile because you were involved with a particular beautiful boy or girl. Young people base their love often on outer attractiveness. Soul love is based on inner attractiveness.

Soul love is not only the love you may feel for another human being. Soul love is a lot broader than that. It is an ongoing feeling of wonder at the beauty of everything around you.

When you look at your life, you may see both aspects of love clearly. When a child is born, it requires unconditional love to survive. Even if the child's parents are not loving, the child will love them. A child also exhibits unconditional love in its constant wonder at and natural acceptance of all it encounters. When people grow up in your society, unfortunately, they become serious and close themselves off from this natural state of unconditional love and acceptance. Happiness is more easily attained in your society when you are in a child-like state than when you are in a grown-up state. To a large extent, being grown-up in your society involves blocking the natural flow. This blocking usually starts early in life when parents tell their child how to perceive the world.

Schools do this in an even more thorough and more exaggerated way. For the most part, schools are institutions designed to develop the mental energy body. We would prefer that your education system placed far greater emphasis on the development of the emotional and the intuitive energy bodies.

In your society, the teaching process places great emphasis on thinking rationally and developing the mental energy body. The teaching process is based primarily on people's fairly rigid mental structures, which are based on fears related to survival. When humans first discovered the information they now teach in schools, it was based on higher love, creativity, and intent. The change is regrettable.

Humanity's fears related to survival limit thinking processes to the rational and mental. The result is that higher love recedes into the background and is replaced by daily love, which only serves personality goals. When you are in an open, child-like state of wonder, you can learn and discover a great deal more about higher aspects of human life such as higher love. As you rediscover this state of child-like wonder, you regain your ability to be open to whatever you may encounter on your path and find new creativity to deal with the world around you.

You may rediscover higher love, creativity, and intent by remembering them as they existed in your own childhood when you were in a much more open state. You can develop these states by looking inward and connecting with your soul.

Daily and higher creativity

Now we will speak more about the distinction between daily forms of creativity and higher forms of creativity.

Daily creativity is the creativity you use to resolve your day-to-day problems and make decisions. *Higher creativity* is the creativity that is present in the universe as a full-flowing energy. Works of art and scientific insights come from the higher level of creativity.

The mental energy body, in combination with the emotional energy body, is a vehicle for reaching states of higher creativity. In order to reach these states, you must first dissolve your rigidities. When you have an open mind, you do not filter the thoughts that come to you. You simply accept each thought as energy with inherent potential.

Grown-ups, especially, have learned to place values on their thoughts to make them fit into the world of divisions. Grown-ups may do this in an extreme way as they judge thoughts as right or wrong. Children do not have such judgments. Children are still in a more natural state in which they perceive every thought—be it loving, aggressive, or otherwise—as energy. Children handle thoughts as energy; they do not restrict the flow of their thoughts by placing judgments on them.

Only a small proportion of your thoughts comes from your own being. Most of your thoughts are energy that flows in from the universe. This energy takes on form when it comes into your mental energy body. A small part of your personality is what most people hope it is, namely something that exists on its own. The major part of your personality is composed of free-flowing energies from the universe. Since your personality greatly wants to be valued for itself, it may feel challenged or frightened when it learns the truth about what most thoughts really are. However, your personality's desire to be valued is just another human survival mechanism. The personality, or ego, fears destruction. It does not know the truth that your true being cannot be destroyed.

Your true self is not the mental part of your being as most people assume. The mental part of your personality, which you consider your ego or identity, is only a small part of your true being. You need the mental part to survive on the earth plane. Unfortunately, you humans have over-emphasized this mental part to such a degree that you overlook the main part of your being: that part which is attuned to the free-flowing energies of the universe.

The way to connect with higher creativity is to open your

mental and emotional energy bodies to tap into the free-flowing energies of the universe. When you do this, you can select the energies which best serve the being that you really are.

As you find higher creativity by bringing more flow into your mental and emotional energy bodies, your ideas are greatly stimulated, your choices become much clearer. Emotional states such as boredom, which you may occasionally experience now, no longer exist. You experience your world as abundant with possibilities. Rather than have no idea about what you are to do, you find it difficult to choose from the many possibilities.

Boredom is also present in what you call depression. In this state of being, you are shut off from your source, from the guidance of your soul, and from the universe. At another time, we may discuss what you call psychiatric diseases because, in one way or another, they all involve being shut off from your unlimited joyful and loving potential. In fact, most so-called psychiatric disorders are conditions in which the personality is shut off in one way or the other from its source of endless love and joyful potential.

Daily and higher intent

Now we will speak about intent. Intent is the direction in which your love and creativity move by using your will. You may differentiate between *daily intent* and *higher intent.*

In your daily life, you use intent to achieve goals, perhaps to create a career or a marriage, or to make money. Daily intent has more to do with survival than with joy and growth.

Intent in its higher form always has to do with joy and growth. You know whether your intention or desire is coming from a higher or lower level by whether or not you experience joy and expansion. The joy we are talking about is not the joy of momentary gratification resulting from daily experiences such as having sexual intercourse, eating a good meal, or watching a nice football game. We are talking here about a deeper joy, a joy that is a state of inner excitement or bliss that you experience when you follow the direction of your soul.

For example, if you envision possibilities for your career, you may experience deep joy. This joy comes from the soul. Along with this joy comes a feeling or a knowing that you are developing your being in ways that are in accord with your talents and potential. This joy is much deeper than the joy you feel at the personality level. You may envision possibilities for your career while your main goal may be to be admired or accepted by others. In that case, your intent will be at the daily level of the personality and not at the higher level of the soul. You will not feel the deep, fulfilling enthusiasm and joy that you experience when your intent is soul-based.

When your intent is high level, your satisfaction and gratification come from inside rather than from outside. This fact may help you to differentiate between daily intent and higher intent.

When you reconnect with your open state of consciousness, you develop your contact with higher love, creativity, intent, and with the Higher Will of the universe.

This is the end of this chapter. For now, we say good-bye to you with all our love and light.

18.
The Power of Thoughts

Mount Shasta, lower slopes

Welcome, this is Phylos. We would now like to discuss the power of your thoughts.

Earlier we stated that only a small proportion of your thoughts come from your physical being, the vehicle you created to live on the earth plane. A far larger proportion of your thoughts are energies that you pick up from the universe. By thoughts, we do not mean only verbal thoughts. Thoughts can also come as pictures, symbols, or sounds. Thoughts are energies, which come from the free-floating energy layers of the universe and condense into your mental energy body. A thought, therefore, is energy from the universe that is condensed. You can learn to manipulate this energy at will, choosing energies and condensing them into thoughts, and further condensing the thoughts into matter and forms of your choice.

Your perception is greatly influenced by your thoughts

Your awareness on the earth plane consists of the input from your senses plus your thoughts. For the most part, your senses perceive the energies which are around you. Your senses can perceive these energies only partially. Your perception of these energies is more fixed than your perception of your thoughts is. Your perception of your outer world is not as easy to manipulate as your perception of your thoughts is.

How you perceive your outer world with your senses depends mostly on your thoughts. However, you are not conscious of this fact. In your perception, a table, for example, remains the same table regardless of the angle from which you look at it, how much light is falling on it, and whether it is nearby or some distance away. By means of thought processes, which began when you were born into the earth plane, you develop a constancy of objects. Actually, the concept of constancy of objects is a deceptive one; in truth, you invent this constancy from moment to moment. A large part of your brain's activity is involved in maintaining your view of the world. The thoughts involved in this process come from your earth body's survival mechanisms.

You can change your perception

You can change your perception. Meditation is one way to do this. A quicker way is to use hallucinogenic drugs. That would show you very quickly how your perceptions can change. But we do not advise you to take hallucinogens since they create harmful imbalances in your energy.

Your thoughts are easier to manipulate than your perception. Your thoughts are a layer of energy which exists between the spiritual dimension and the earth dimension. The thoughts that come from your inner being form the greatest part of your thought processes. These thoughts also determine how you perceive your world and what you perceive in your world. Therefore, if you change your thoughts, your perception of the world changes. If your perception of the world changes, your world itself starts to change in a very real sense. You create your own world with your thoughts.

You create your reality with your thoughts; you perceive that reality with your senses. You have perceptual mechanisms with which you interpret the input from your senses. You may consider these perceptual mechanisms as specific kinds of thought processes. These thought processes are more difficult to change than your regular thoughts are.

If you change your thoughts, your perception of your sensory input changes too. You may experience this after meditation, for example, when you feel very open and you notice that colors look brighter.

To change what your senses perceive is difficult. The thoughts that make up your world are the result of a lifelong process of reinforcing the same vision. You can, however, completely change the input from your senses and begin to see things as energy patterns. This, however, requires a lot of skill.

Be conscious about where you place your awareness

You create your world with your daily thoughts and visions as well as with your higher thoughts and visions. Your thoughts play a powerful role in determining your reality so be very conscious of what you are thinking.

Most of your thinking is unconscious. You are, for example, not conscious of the language you use and share with all the people in your community. People who use different languages have different perceptions of the world. If your only word for little flying feathered animals is birds, you will have difficulty distinguishing between different kinds of birds.

When you study many kinds of birds and the differences in their songs, you will begin to recognize and actually see more kinds of birds.

When you bring more of your awareness to any one kind of thing, perhaps a material thing like a car, or a quality like violence, or an emotion like love, the same thing happens. The more awareness you put into a particular subject, the more it appears in your reality.

Consciously or unconsciously, you create your own reality by choosing where to place your awareness. For example, if you are obsessed with health, you may focus continually on ways to stay healthy and be preoccupied all day long with hygiene, diet, and exercise. But you will create illness instead of health because your awareness is unconsciously focused on your fear of illness. If you keep your precautions against illness at a low level and just believe that you will be healthy regardless of the circumstances, you are far more likely to be healthy.

Free yourself from mass thinking

You share a world perspective with all those people with whom you share a language. Language is based on many underlying and mostly unconscious assumptions about what reality is like. All of you who speak a common language maintain the illusion that your perception of the world is real, and each of you believes you can verify your perception because other people share it. If you see a flying saucer and your neighbors see it too, you are convinced that it is real. On the other hand, if your neighbors do not see it, if you are the only one seeing it, you may think you are going crazy.

This mass thinking is one way in which you maintain the illusion that the world you perceive is real. In order to become free in how you think and how you create your world, you must free yourself from the processes of mass thinking. Of course, you will find it difficult to change your language altogether. Some schizophrenic people, however, may develop a whole new language and with that a whole new set of perceptions. But they may find this experience undesirable since it does not involve communication with their source. If, however, you consciously free yourself from mass thinking, you can create profound changes in your reality. Then enlightenment is within your reach.

When you refrain from participating in the mass thinking process, you become free to create your world in your own way. We recommend that you start creating your world aligned with the purposes of your soul and the Higher Will.

You can choose to live in the reality of your soul

You might think of the universe as a sea of different energies and potentials. Many different combinations of these energies and potentials are possible. You can bring all the qualities and forms you desire into your reality when you develop your ability to elevate your consciousness to the level of the sea of energy and potential.

Next, by using the forces of love, creativity, and intent, you can condense the free-floating energies of potential at will. First they condense into the form of thoughts. When you charge your thoughts with love, creativity, and intent, your thoughts may condense further into denser forms, qualities, and matter. You do this all the time, although you are usually not consciously aware of this. By using your love, creativity, and intent consciously, you can create at will the changes you desire in your reality.

You will find it easy to manifest that forms that are truly desired by your soul or by the higher forces of the universe. You will find it more difficult to manifest forms that are based mostly on your personality's desires. Forms that are in alignment with your soul and with the universe are easier to create because they are aligned with the forces of higher love, creativity, and intent. For example, your personality may wish to buy an expensive car. That desire may contain a lot of intent but may not be aligned with your higher path or with love. This form will not appear in your reality easily. But if the car comes into your life easily, for example, if you wanted it and then won it in a lottery, probably your having the car serves a higher purpose for your soul.

You can manipulate forms and create them more quickly when you bring your consciousness up to the level of the sea of energy of potential. One way of doing this is to meditate. The other way is to change your thoughts.

You create your world with your thoughts. Therefore, if you want to live in a happy world, have happy thoughts about the world. Think happy thoughts about yourself and about others. As much as possible, think about yourself, your goals, and other people in positive ways.

People sometimes find it hard to comprehend that thoughts have such enormous manifesting power. One single thought generally will not manifest in your life immediately because it is only one thought in a sea of other positive and negative thoughts. Your positive and negative thoughts are balanced in a way that keeps your world the way it is. If you start to change your thoughts in a consistent way, you will find that your world will change quite rapidly.

Your first step toward enlightenment in this lifetime is to make conscious contact with your soul and with the universe.

EARTH CHANGES

You can accomplish this with meditation. Your second step is to change your thoughts. When you consistently change your thoughts into positive ones, your life will change rapidly in a positive way.

Speak positively about yourself and others

For example, if you have mixed feelings about a friend, you may talk about negative things about this friend. As you focus on his negative aspects, you reinforce them. If, on the other hand, you concentrate on your friend's beauty and other fine qualities, if you are compassionate and understanding and try to see the world through his eyes, you empower him and help clear any discord between you.

If, like Froukje and Jeroen, you have a housekeeper whom others have called a thief, and you constantly talk about and think of her as a thief, you are creating the thief in her. If, however, you break away from this type of mass thinking and start to talk and think positively about her, holding a vision that she is a good soul, she will not steal in your house. We cannot say that she will never steal again. Other people may still think and talk negatively about her thereby impacting her behavior.

Phylos's example comes out of our personal experience. Shortly after a housekeeper started working for us, we heard that she was a thief and a liar, and that we should be very careful with her. We decided to give her a chance and held a positive image of her. We never hid things from her and we gave her the key to our house. She has been working for us for two years and we have never missed anything. In fact, often she brought us flowers when we returned home after a long trip. We tried to pay her for taking care of our dog while we were away, but she refused payment insisting that she had cared for him out of love.

The process of creating with your thoughts is complicated by the fact that you are not the only creator in this world. Group energy influences your process of creating. However, when you start thinking and speaking positively yourself, your example may have a spin-off effect on others and change the group energy. Let us stay with the example of the housekeeper. If you tell the people who told you that she is a thief that she is really very nice, that she takes good care of your dog and your house, their thoughts about her may start to change. Positive ways of thinking and speaking are very powerful. When you think about your housekeeper in a high way you may change her in a very real way. Since she feels happy with you, the factors that once caused her to steal may leave her energy field, allowing her to learn to trust more and be honest with people.

This principle also applies on the concrete level of matter. Since your thoughts are manifestations of energy condensed from the sea of potential in the universe, they have the potential to create real forms. Thoughts are so powerful that they can create concrete material things in your world. If you truly desire a material object, you may focus your thoughts toward getting it. If your desire is an honest one and is in alignment with your higher purpose, the possibility that it will manifest in your life is quite real. If you think consistently about having a thing, and about what good it will do for you and for others, it will manifest quite easily in your life.

Be persistent in your efforts to think positively

This process may be complicated, however, by mass

thought forms, which you have incorporated and which are contrary to your desire to be positive. At first you may find it a real effort to think positively, feel worthy, and refrain from doubting your manifesting abilities. Your doubts may persist for a while, but if you persist in changing them to the thoughts you really want, not only may your wish come true, but also your whole world may change.

It is important to discover to what degree mass thinking has become part of your own thinking. Compare how you think and how your society wants you to think. For example, most people believe that a murderer must be severely punished. If he is not, many of you will wish for revenge or punishment, or at least you will feel that justice has not been done. The concept that a murderer should not be punished may be an example of a new thought for you. Murderers should not be punished at all. Punishment creates negative energy and even more negative thoughts in the murderer. Punishment also creates more fear for people who want murderers to be punished, thus creating more murderers. Ideally, you would not create murderers in the first place, but since they do exist in your society they should be treated with love, however difficult this may be for you.

This is just one example of a mass thought form that you may have incorporated. Our suggestion about changing this thought form might challenge you. Of course, there are many more such examples.

You might refrain from mass media for a while

All day long you are bombarded with information from your society. The mass media especially creates a way of mass thinking that may be undesirable for your own development and that of humanity as a whole.

When you become conscious of the way in which you incorporate mass thinking, you are able to step out of it. You may find it helpful to remove your attention from the mass media. If you read newspapers or watch television, we would suggest that you stop doing that, at least for a while.

If you feel resistant to this idea, you may notice that we are touching upon another mass idea, namely the belief that you should stay informed about the news. Most of you have been raised with the idea that you should be interested in politics and that you should read newspapers. All shoulds are mass thought processes that you have internalized.

We are not suggesting that you live outside your society or that you avoid all newspapers and television. We are suggesting that you might refrain from these things just for a while in order to become conscious of the way mass thinking impacts you and of the fact that you are mostly not conscious of this. By distancing yourself from the news, you can increase your ability to see how and how much the media influences you. And you can sharpen your ability to see through mass thought forms.

Perhaps you have a special interest in politics. Especially if your higher purpose is to become a politician, the best thing for your development might be to stop reading and hearing about politics for a while. When we say a while, we mean a period from one to six months, or longer. During this period, you may discover which ideas are your own, that is, come from your inner being, and which ideas are based on mass thinking. Powerful mass thought forms define a good politician as someone who is a strong debater and who takes a firm stand on issues. But when you no longer allow the media to influence you, you may develop a higher vision about what constitutes a good politician. Your vision may differ greatly from that which is created by mass thought forms.

Positive thoughts held by a group of people have tremendous power

A powerful way to change mass thinking is to create a positive vision with a group of people. In the example of the housekeeper, we saw how the people around her believed she was a thief, spoke of her as such, and therefore actually caused and reinforced her stealing behavior. We also saw how positive thoughts can have positive spin-offs and are a great deal more powerful than negative thoughts are. These statements are true because positive thinking is in alignment with the love, creativity, and intent of the universe, and in alignment with Higher Will.

When you combine your positive thinking with other people's, you really can create a strong force field and change a whole society. When you come together as a group and hold a positive vision—one inspired by high qualities from your soul like love, harmony, beauty, and oneness—you may send this vision out into the world. That way, you are changing the mass thinking of your society in a powerful way. As a rule of thumb, you might say that one percent can change one hundred percent. However, do not take these figures too literally because many other factors such as the quality of your thoughts are also involved.

This is the end of the chapter. For now, we say good-bye to you with all our love and light.

19.
Selfishness

Mount Shasta

Welcome, this is Phylos. In this chapter we will discuss selfishness. When we talk about living on this planet, we can talk about two modes of living: *daily life* or *earthly life*, and *spiritual life*. One of your main purposes for being here is to blend these two.

Learn to distinguish between your personality's motives and your soul's motives

Many people want to be helpful to others. This desire to help and to hold a focus for the growth of others may be a beautiful expression of a soul wish which is rooted in a deep feeling of compassion. Unfortunately, teachers and other helpers are often motivated by earthly purposes, that is, the purposes of their personalities. A helper may desire love from those he serves, or acknowledgment for helping.

If you teach, you may have an unconscious wish to force your beliefs and values upon others. Hidden personality goals may also find their expression in channeling. We talked earlier about such difficulties in channeling. A good channel has to be clear about his purposes. Naturally Jeroen's personality would like to see this book sell in many bookstores and may have fantasies about being interviewed and receiving other public acknowledgment. These desires and fantasies come from his personality. They are not necessarily consistent with our goals as we speak through him.

Read or listen to channeled information with your intuition. If, for example, someone who is channeling a guide tells you what you should or should not do, be aware that the channel's personality issues may be involved. We hope that this material will be relatively free of such distortions, but we cannot avoid them completely.

Helping or teaching can serve a high purpose, but you have to be clear about your purposes and at least be conscious of the possibility that personality issues might be involved.

If you want to help others, you need to help yourself first

We named this chapter *Selfishness* to challenge you a bit. We recommend that you become more selfish by making self-love and self-care your first priority. Loving yourself and taking good care of yourself also implies investigating your motives and goals. We hope you will not read this as a should, however. Helping people even when you are not in a high state of purity is just fine.

We recommend, however, that you work on your personality issues to become clearer about your motives and goals. If you are confused about your real motives and goals, your life may be troublesome. You may be unconscious of the fact that you are pretending to be more evolved than you really are. For example, some teachers may behave like gurus but not possess a *real* guru's humility and knowledge of spiritual truth. Adapt your actions to your level of growth at any given time.

Usually the universe works in such a way that you naturally function at the level of your present growth. However, you may easily loose your balance and feel yourself a little bigger than you really are, especially if you are working in a field in which you are helping others.

When you help others, do not expect anything in return

The word selfishness has a negative connotation in mass thinking. When you look at selfishness more closely, you will see that the best way to help others and the world is by creating the best you can for yourself. If you want to help others primarily because you want to be loved yourself, the love you send out to the other person is not deep or genuine.

You may have had some experiences with this kind of situation. Perhaps someone helped you, and you were grateful for his help. But receiving his help did not cause you to feel more love for him. Later, you may have sensed that he felt disappointed or resentful because you did not love him more. His hidden motive for offering you help may have been to get more love or recognition from you.

You can only be of real help to another if you do not want anything in return, at least not on a psychological level. However, energy exchanges on other levels should be more or less equal. Asking for money in return for your help is fine, but expecting love in return is not wise.

If you help another person because you feel compassion for him and do not demand anything for yourself in return, you may be surprised to receive much love in return. You will accept this love with gratitude and not out of need. However, if your motive for helping is to be loved, the love you get back will not satisfy your need for love. You cannot buy real love. We hesitate to use the word buy. After all, your conscious intentions were not bad. But you were just not conscious of your true intentions.

Be selfish. Take time to love yourself and to connect with your soul and with the higher forces of the universe. I guarantee that the deepest love and compassion will open for you, and you will move into a nondemanding, peaceful state from which you can reach out to the world. If you open yourself to our love and to the universe's love, you also learn to love yourself more deeply.

Learn to love yourself more

You can learn to love yourself more on two levels: the level of your every day life and the level of your spiritual life. On the spiritual level, you can meditate to connect with your soul and the higher forces of the universe.

I will talk a bit more now about how to increase self-love at the level of every day life.

You all have a basic need for love. If you want to receive more love from others, start by changing your thoughts about yourself. This is the first way to increase self-love. You might do this exercise: Make a list of everything you like about yourself. List all your good qualities. Add to your list every day. Working on this list is a good way to change your thoughts about yourself and to become more loving towards yourself.

A second way to increase your self-love at the level of everyday life is to recognize and honor the free child within you. When you listen to the needs of this inner child, you have more clarity about what is good for you. Your free child's choices are flexible. Rigid choices tend not to be loving to the self. A child who has already incorporated his parents' and other educators' shoulds and don'ts, a child who behaves in rigid ways and who is strict with himself is not the free child I am talking about. The free child within you is the child who knows exactly how to take good care of you.

Perhaps your inner child wants things that you think you should not have like cookies, new clothes, toys, or whatever. We are not proposing that you do things that do not support your higher good. However, when your inner child wants cookies, we would advise you to buy the most delicious and expensive cookies you can find. This is a good way of spending your money. Spending money on your inner child's needs is sometimes more important than for example donate money to a good cause.

A third way to increase your self-love is to allow yourself to feel all your feelings. During your upbringing, you learned to suppress most of your feelings. The free child within you allows all of its feelings and expresses them in any way it wants.

Do not judge your feelings

Try not to judge your feelings. If you are envious of someone, accept that feeling and let it be there. Really let go of your judgment about any feelings you may have. Be happy that you can feel so intensely. If you welcome every feeling, whatever its nature, you will notice that you start feeling more. The result will be more feelings of love and joy, and ultimately of deep inner peace.

In addition, you will learn that feeling anger and sadness is not bad. Mostly what makes these feelings bad for you is that you fear them. You might fear the damage that your anger may bring about, or you might fear that your sadness will never end. But if you just let these feelings be, you will soon notice that you are feeling them for shorter periods. Your anger and sadness will stop and when they do, you will have more room for joy, peace, happiness, love, and any other higher soul qualities you can conceive of. You may even enjoy your angry, envious, and sad feelings, and learn to play with them.

You can change your thoughts about yourself into more positive ones. You can also let your emotions be whatever they are. For the most part, you can take these steps by yourself, or at least get a good start on them.

People often fear that others will not love them, or find them attractive, or interesting to talk with, or desirable to relate to. You are interesting, loveable, and worthwhile. This statement applies to all of you without exception. Every soul is loveable, interesting, and worthwhile. Your fears do not exist on the level of your soul. Fear is an emotion that is part of the survival mechanisms of the earth plane. Fear has nothing to do with your true being.

You are lovable as you are

Children can be manipulated with fear. In more or less subtle ways, adults often manipulate children to control them. The only kind of fear a free child knows is the fear required to survive life-threatening danger.

Fear that others will not love you, consider you attractive, or find you worthy of friendship is not that kind of fear. Society manipulates people, consciously or unconsciously, to feel this kind of fear. When you were born into this world, you were loveable. Do you know any infant that is not loveable? So how could it be that you are the only infant that is not loveable? Of course, you were loveable as an infant and you still are.

When you read this, all kinds of negative self-talk may come up, like: Yes, but I am not attractive. I am too fat. I have pimples. You may come up with many reasons for finding yourself unattractive. You may think that you have nothing to say, or that you have not studied enough, or you may doubt yourself in some other way. Recognize all of these beliefs as important parts of your personality. Recognize also that they are based on fear and are not a true reflection of the person that you are. If you look around, you will see people who seem too fat, or too thin, or who have pimples—who are nevertheless loveable, have good relationships, and love themselves. You will also see people who do not talk or listen much, yet they are loveable and their company is pleasurable.

I will not try to convince you of this because, if you doubt yourself, I am sure that you will find a way to conclude that my words do not apply to you. If this is true, probably your fears were induced early in your life and you created an image of yourself as unlovable.

Possibly your negative self image is reflected in your physical form and behavior. Perhaps you might really want to loose or gain some weight, or let yourself be heard more. If so, you can make these changes relatively easily once you start loving yourself more.

Other people do not see you the way you see yourself. People do not judge you as being fat or thin, or having pimples, or being too silent, or too talkative, and so on. If they seem to, it is because they reflect your negative self-image back to you. At a deep level, all people want to love and to be loved. Everyone is insecure; you are certainly no exception. This is as true for you as for anyone else. When you connect with the free child within—the inner child that feels no limitations—you connect with your true, loving, and playful self. The free child does not share your insecurities.

If you do not believe that you are lovable, pretend that you are

The fourth way to learn to become more selfish is to release your fear of unworthiness by behaving *as though* you are loveable, worthwhile, and interesting. Pretending is a powerful way to change your thoughts about yourself. Your reality, and even the physical forms in your reality will change when you pretend you are worthwhile. You may not be able to do this all at once. You may start today by writing down one positive thing about yourself and by doing one thing that your inner child would love to do for itself. These processes might help you feel more worthwhile. Pretending that you are worthwhile and writing down one positive thing about yourself is the first step in improving your self-esteem, and a big step. It is a big step because if you can take one step, you can also take the second step, and many more steps thereafter.

Perhaps you feel that these words do not really apply to you. Maybe you are already at a level of growth and self-love where you no longer feel a need for these words. However, we feel that most humans are so involved in mass thinking that they do not value themselves for who they really are. Even if you already love yourself, I would recommend that you do these processes anyway. You can always find a deeper level of self-love and a greater sense of joy and abundance in your life.

This is the end of this chapter. For now, we say good-bye to you with all our love and light.

20.
Meditation: Visiting the Higher Realms

Mount Shasta, higher slopes

Welcome, this is Phylos.

Imagine that you feel the energy, the peace, and the potential of our great mountain, and of our energy and our light.

1. Now focus on your breath. Each breath contains higher energies, and you can expand into them. Your awareness is spreading out in all directions. With each breath, relax a bit more, adjusting your posture.

2. Imagine that there is an opening in the top of your head. Extending upward from this opening is a cone with its apex pointing down. With your inner vision, look up into that cone and move up into it. You are now looking into the higher dimensions, and you may see or feel higher energies with your inner eyes. Maybe you see colors or light. Notice the beauty here.

3. When you become very quiet, you may hear a call from above, as though you are hearing someone call your name in a soft, loving way, inviting you to come up just for a while, to take a look at what is up there.

4. As you respond to the call, you may feel as if you are slowly flowing upward, as if your awareness is leaving your body through the top of your head. All around you is a beautiful

light. You are drifting upward in a sea of the purest and finest light you can imagine. Feel how the light carries you, how it soothes you. Feel the love that is emanating from this light. As you go higher, the light becomes even more beautiful. Watch the colors and the bright, twinkling light.

Notice from the corners of your eyes beings who accompany you as you float upward. Feel the love these beings have for you, and how happy they are that you are connecting with their dimension in this way. They help you find the right direction. Notice that you pass many layers and filters of light as you drift up.

5. As you continue to go higher, you again hear your name being called. This time the call is much closer, and you may hear soft music as you approach the beautiful being that is calling you. You are now close enough to see to this being. You may hear soft, angelic music as you move even closer to the being.

Do not worry if you do not see or hear anything. Just imagine that you sense the presence of this beautiful being, and that you see or sense its radiance, its light and love welcoming you to this dimension. This being may feel very familiar to you; it has been with you often—both while you were awake and while you were asleep. You have met this great being of light on many occasions. In fact, it is always there to remind you of your own greatness. At this level of light, you are a wonderful being of light yourself.

6. Now the being starts talking to you. Quiet your thoughts and emotions as you listen to its words. If you do not hear words, just open to receive the love and support which this beautiful being of light radiates to you. The being invites you to explore its dimension.

7. The being works with your energy for a while, lifting

some of the veils from your inner senses so you can see more clearly into this dimension. Perhaps you have felt you were in a fog. Notice how that fog is clearing now, how the sun is shining through it. Your view is becoming clearer and clearer.

8. When you look around, you may perceive other beings. Feel your senses opening; feel how you are connecting with this world more and more. Notice all the ways in which you perceive this world. Maybe you see pictures, or energies. Pay attention to your feelings too, to how connected you feel to this world.

Notice how all these beings accept you just as you are. They know who you are. They know you are a great being of light. You have been here on many occasions when you were not in your daily consciousness, but you probably do not remember those occasions. These entities are glad that you are here now in a more conscious way so you can take the memory of these encounters back into your daily life more easily.

9. Before you come back, take a few moments to see if there is something you want to do, say, give, or receive.

10. When you are ready, prepare to leave this wonderful place. Notice that the beings who helped you find your way up here are still with you. Now they accompany you back. Feel the love radiating from these beings, blessing you on your way back.

11. Now move back down into your body again through this cone of energy. Feel how you are charged with higher energy. You are now in contact with the loving being you truly are. Come back into your body completely now, feeling clearly your connection with the earth. Feel your physical body's connection with the earth and with gravity. When you are ready, open your eyes, and keep this soft, loving feeling with you for the rest of the day, and maybe even longer. Radiate it to everyone you see or think of.

JEROEN KUYPER

Come back now fully and completely. We say good-bye to you for now with all our love and light.

21.
Exercise: Expanding Consciousness
Mount Shasta, higher slopes

We had arrived at Mount Shasta City more than a week ago. The day we arrived, the newspaper reported a record rainfall. Camping seemed impossible, so we had rented a cabin at the campground in Mount Shasta City. We had been walking high up on the mountain where snow was falling because we preferred walking in snow to walking in rain.

Today, finally, the weather was clearing up. We were in very different moods. Froukje felt energetic and wanted to move to the campground at the lake. However, I felt very tired, almost ill. While walking in the snow, I recovered quickly. Meanwhile, Froukje's energy dropped unexpectedly. We decided to stay in the cabin for one more night.

This is Phylos. We welcome you to our realms, and we suggest you take a moment to stop and feel the presence of the beings of light here. Although we are in a different realm, we greet you today by asking the birds to do so. They are by nature more open to contact with our realms than you human beings are. Listen to their welcome now.

What happened to you today was this: Both of your flows collapsed, each at a different time. You were obviously not in the same flow. Earlier today, Froukje was in a phase of new energy and new ideas, and Jeroen was in a phase of recharging. Now we see that Jeroen has recharged quite a lot, while Froukje has not yet found a way to use the energies here and is feeling some numbness. You can recharge quite quickly by walking in the snow in this highly energized environment. We suggest that you do not walk too fast; allow yourself to feel the energies of the surroundings.

So start by walking slowly. You can expand your consciousness by taking every step in a conscious way and by absorbing more of the energies here with every step you take. Widen the scope of your vision and look up rather than down at the ground. In this way, you absorb more energy.

When you look up, do not concentrate on the center of your vision but on the periphery of it. Looking in this way expands your consciousness. Your eyes play an important role in accessing different states of consciousness. Your eyes also play a part in the use of your inner senses. The movements of your eyes and the direction in which they turn have important consequences for your state of consciousness.

Normally when you look, you use primarily the center of your vision. Humans are conditioned to focusing on the center of their vision. When you walk slowly and use the periphery of your vision, you can see much more and increasingly expand your vision. For example, now try to look at what you see on the outer edges of both sides of your field of vision. Keep your eyes focused, but in a kind of soft focus, while you look with your peripheral vision. You may already have felt a shift in your energy by just focusing this way. You may have noticed that it was easier to tap into the energies about you. You may perceive a deepening of the colors and the beauty you are experiencing.

Now hold all this in your attention and at the same time be aware of the movement of your body and of the contact you feel with the earth with every step you take.

We suggest that you stop for a while now and close your eyes. Just feel the energy.

A being of light is preparing to help you sense even more energy. This being has descended into your world. Sense where this being is and how it moves. Feel its energy in your energy field as it moves to a different position now. Observe that your eyes are naturally turning in that direction.

After this exercise, that took about five minutes, Phylos continued.

Now open your eyes again. You may start walking again if you wish. This exercise helps you to recognize more of the energies around you and to learn to see energies around people. Perhaps you noticed that you could sense the beings of light more easily during this exercise than you could before.

***

P: Where do you spot this being?

F: I feel it there between the trees.

P: That is correct. See or feel how it appears to you. You may walk toward this being and sense whether you can feel the changes in your energy while you walk through its energy fields. As you can see, this being has no problem with the snow.

While walking to the place where we sensed the being, we sank one to two feet into the snow with every step.

***

Later that day, when we were back in our cabin at the campground in Mount Shasta City, we had some personal questions for Phylos. We include these questions and his elaborate answers because we feel they contain some interesting processes and viewpoints.

Making decisions using joy as a sense

F: I feel that I am closer to having a baby. Can you say something about that?

P: You have a question about something important in your life. First, you might see if you are perhaps somewhat ambivalent. What is most important in this decision is the amount of joy you get from the images you have about bringing a child into your life. Again, it is important to distinguish between your daily thoughts, and your higher thoughts and feelings about what you might want to create. In this matter of bringing a child into your life, a good measure to go by is the feelings you get when you picture yourself having a little child. Will it give you joy? Will it provide you with a focus upon which to put your radiance and your love? These are the important issues. When you look at the possibilities from the earth level, mostly rational thoughts come up, like: Will I be able to do my work if I have a child? Will a child be too demanding for me? Will it cry too much? Maybe other fear-based, rational thoughts also arise.

When you live your life in the higher flow of the universe, you do not let these thoughts guide you. Your guidance is the feeling you have deep inside you. You may connect with that feeling now. You can feel a yes or a no at a deep level.

We will now do a little exercise to help you to find an answer to your question. Close your eyes and relax. Let yourself expand more into a quiet, peaceful state, relaxing the muscles in your neck.

Picture yourself holding a baby right here and now. See

the baby, the head, the fingers, the toes, and its whole little body. Feel its movement and feel how you feel about holding the baby in your arms. Feel your connection with this child. How does this connection feel? What do you want to do with the child?

You may also picture yourself with your child while it is growing up, while it requires a lot of attention and care. When the child cries or screams, what do you do? Do you still feel joy and love?

You may come back now with a felt sense about whether the time is right to have a child.

When you base all the decisions in your life upon rational thinking, tallying up all the pros and cons in each situation, you will find that you get tired of all this balancing and waiting. You can create a better life by just following the higher flow. When you feel a yes, act. The consequences of your yes are always the right consequences. Of course, you may encounter difficulties on your path regardless of which choice you make. The possible negative consequences will be moderate if you follow your heart's choice; the difficulties you encounter will always be lessons to help you with your growth. If, however, you make a decision that is not based upon a deep felt sense or upon a message from your soul, you will encounter far more difficult challenges and lessons.

Do you have more questions about this or about something else?

Learn to remember what you came to do

F: Can you say something about what happens when a soul wants to incarnate?

P: The soul is conscious of its origins when it first enters physical life on the earth. The soul knows its parents as beings of light and is open and loving toward everything in the environment.

Sometimes the soul chooses a loving, easygoing childhood. Sometimes, for purposes of its own, it chooses a more difficult childhood. In your case, your soul chose a difficult childhood so you could develop certain qualities. When a child is loved and well-nourished, it does not develop as much fear and rigidity as might be the case when the circumstances are difficult. You chose to receive a lot of love at a very young age while your father was still alive. You knew that you needed a loving start so that you would be able to learn from the period of loneliness and lack of love that followed. Your childhood was not totally lacking in love, nevertheless, the circumstances were difficult.

When you are in this earth life, you soon forget the decisions you made as a soul before you came to the earth. Beings like me give guidance to help you stay in an open state for longer periods, to help you remember your reasons for coming here. You humans can also teach your children to stay open longer. As it is now, children soon forget what they came here to do and what their purpose is.

You all need many lessons to rediscover your higher path. The pressures and difficulties you encounter in your life let you know that you are out of the higher flow and no longer following your higher path. The uncomfortable feelings that these pressures and difficulties give you are your soul's signals to you that you are off your higher path. If you could not feel these discomforts, your soul could not tell you that you are taking a wrong turn. Some people have trained themselves, willingly or unwillingly, to neglect the soul's signals. Such neglect often leads people into the state you call burnout.

When you are not on your higher path, you feel

something is missing from your life. You do not experience much joy. You may try to compensate for your lack of love and joy with substitutes like alcohol or drugs. Or you may develop a successful career in order to feel recognized. But if you are not on your higher path, your feeling of lack remains regardless of what you do. For example, you may have a successful career but still feel lonely. However, if you have a successful career based on your higher path, you feel fulfilled, energetic, enthusiastic, and loved.

Depression is a wonderful learning opportunity

P: Feelings of depression are also a sign that you are not on your higher path. Sometimes depressed people have no contact with their soul anymore. This happens when they are so depressed that they complain about having no feelings at all.

Emotions are mainly messages from your soul, guiding you in a certain direction. In your case, Froukje, you once had a period of little soul contact, but not a total lack of soul contact. You were off your higher path, however.

You can learn a lot from such episodes. When you look back, you will notice that you certainly feel wiser now than you felt before that period. When you are depressed, you connect with the depths of life itself, and that is the function of depression. Mostly, people consider depression to be a negative state, but in fact, it is a beautiful one. The more depressed you are, the more you encounter the basic issues of your existence, and with that the sense and purpose of your life on earth.

For many people, a period of depression may be the first time they encounter the deeper levels of existence. When you are depressed, you may grow and find your higher path again by seeking guidance or by doing things that are good for you.

When you are not on your soul's higher path, you might be depressed and have physical complaints. These are often your soul's messages that tell you that something is not as it should be. Your emotions and physical sensations are necessary—your soul uses them to communicate with you. Even when you are on a higher path, as you are now, emotions and physical complaints may persist, telling you there is more to learn, more to resolve.

Do you have any questions about this?

F: Are you saying that my physical complaints help me connect more with my higher path?

P: You do not need those kinds of lessons anymore. You already have a clearer vision of your higher path. You can see that the things you are doing now are far beyond your vision of what was possible during your period of depression. You needed quite a lot of depression to find your higher path again. Since you have now learned how to stay on your higher path and follow the subtle signs of your soul, you no longer need physical symptoms or strong emotions to accomplish this. If physical symptoms or strong emotions persist or return, they mostly serve the function of resolving past trauma.

The amount of pain or emotion you feel now is partly a function of how much you once suppressed your pain or emotion. Let me explain this from an energy perspective. A childhood trauma like the loss of your father could have caused a drastic shrinking of your energy fields. Strong emotions may have given you the boost of energy you required to rebuild your collapsed energies. The sadness you felt and still feel about the loss of your father helped and still helps you clear the entanglements and points in your energy bodies that are not yet flowing freely. What you call sadness is, in fact, a freeing of the stream of love, of the ability to feel love again. Crying results from the mingling of pain and love—the pain you feel when the knots in your energy bodies untangle and the deep love you feel for the soul that is your father.

If your energy fields have shrunk a lot, especially if this happened at an early age, you may experience intense physical symptoms. These may take quite a while to overcome. In fact, when you first free your emotional energy body, they may become even worse. In the process of your growth, do not be discouraged if you have physical complaints that seem to last forever. Treat them with love and patience.

Do you have any more questions?

F: No, not at this moment.

P: Then we will close this session, thanking you for your support. We thank you for your love, we thank you for your being, and we say good-bye to you for now.

22.
Building Consciousness
Upper Mount Shasta

Welcome, this is Phylos. We greet you from our realms high up on our mountain. We send you our love and support. We now begin this chapter about building consciousness.

One way to build consciousness is by doing exercises that stretch your perception. By doing such exercises, you will find that your senses expand and sharpen. Your intuition will develop while your intuitive energy body grows.

Gaining consciousness is part of your life purpose

To live on the earth plane, you must adapt to the conditions here. When you leave the free-flowing consciousness state of our realms to incarnate onto the earth plane, you have to adapt to the denser energy forms of the earth. Your mastery of the earth plane serves primarily to help you regain consciousness of our realms. The more consciousness you regain, the easier it is for you to re-establish your connection with these realms. Gaining consciousness means that you are becoming more aware of the totality of your consciousness. And gaining consciousness means that you are finding the doorways to other realms and realities.

Why should you expand your consciousness in this way? The essence of consciousness is that it wants to develop itself. The more you develop your consciousness, the more joy, peace, and harmony you experience. You may also gain greater balance within your true being and more connection with the higher forces of the universe. On the earth plane, you may experience harmony, love, health, and energy in your physical body.

You can gain consciousness on two different levels. The first level is the earthly one. The second level is that of the higher realms: you can reach out to these realms directly, using meditation and your inner senses.

In this chapter, we will talk about the first, earthly way of gaining consciousness. We have already taught you some exercises in which you use your senses and your mental energy body to expand your consciousness. For example, we suggested that when you eat you be fully aware of your process and your taste experience. We also suggested that you use your peripheral vision to expand your larger vision. And we suggested that you be conscious of every step you take. These exercises employ your earthly senses to expand your consciousness. They help you live your daily life with as much consciousness as possible.

To expand your consciousness, love yourself and take good care of yourself

We will now talk about other earthly ways to expand your consciousness.

Sometimes you are so busy with so many things at the same time that you cannot concentrate well. Other times you are very quiet and focused, and do things step by step. You tend to function better and at a higher level when you are in the latter state. In that state your consciousness expands.

In order to gain more consciousness at the earthly level, take good care of yourself. You might put more care into how and what you eat, and start eating healthier foods. In addition, you might eat slowly and with full concentration.

Physical movement is also an important aspect of self-care. Movement is important to keep your body in good shape. When your are in good physical condition, your consciousness expands more easily than when you are not. If you do not already have a form of movement that promotes the well-being of your body, find one. Examples of good exercises are yoga, Tai Chi, or the exercises that Froukje and Jeroen practice: the Five Tibetans, and the Energization Exercises of Paramahansa Yogananda. Find your own exercises, choosing those that are good for you and that give you a maximum of joy.

We also recommend that you create an environment and do a job that is in harmony with the being that you are. When you do the things you love, your consciousness automatically expands. When you do things you do not enjoy, your consciousness contracts. Crowded places like cities, which contain few natural environments, hinder the expansion of your consciousness. Your consciousness expands naturally when you are out in nature, so we recommend spending a lot of time in nature.

Use joy to change your habits

Many people know intuitively that following the above recommendations promotes health but may not think that following them also promotes consciousness. Many people try repeatedly to change a habit. But often they fall back into their old habit and do not succeed. These people may wonder about how to change their habits to become healthy and more conscious. Again, the key word is *joy*. Joylessly fighting a habit does not change it. If you want to change a habit, start by practicing self-love as we described in chapter twelve.

Next, hold a vision of what you will gain by replacing this habit. The clearer and more joyful your vision about your potential gains, the more easily you will get rid of it. For example, if you want to quit smoking, do not visualize yourself as becoming unhealthy, perhaps getting cancer from smoking. That would be acting out of fear. The process of breaking your habit in this way might be worse for your health than the habit itself is.

Only drop a bad habit when you feel good about doing so. If you want to quit smoking, focus on joyful results: an improved sense of smell and taste, deeper breathing, and a more pleasant taste in your mouth in the morning. Also use visualization: see your physical condition improving enormously and your consciousness expanding. When you have a clear vision about the results you desire, the process of quitting will be a lot easier. As you can see, the key words are *joy* and *self-love*.

When you change a habit, be sure that whatever you are replacing it with is good for you from your soul's perspective. For example, if you eat candies all day long and you are too fat, you might imagine that following a strict diet would be good for you. But a particular diet that might be good for others might not be good for you. Sense how much joy you feel when you think about the diet. Take time to think or meditate about what you will gain by changing your habit and what you will put into its place. Also meditate on the benefits you now receive by having the habit. If you drink alcohol to feel self-assured, explore other ways to create self-assurance. If eating chocolate nourishes you emotionally, imagine alternative ways to nurture and love yourself.

The same applies to physical movement. Be sure that your soul and higher self like the changes you want to make. If you start power lifting or jogging when it is not in alignment with your soul, you will not benefit from it at all. In fact, it may even be harmful for you.

Each person's health needs are unique

Be aware that how the larger society thinks greatly influences your perception of health issues—and, with that, your health itself. Mass thinking about health and exercise is often harmful to your health. Mass thinking can restrict your consciousness rather than expand it. And, if you don't meet your own unique needs regarding diet and exercise, you can also restrict your health.

We cannot give universally applicable guidelines about eating, drinking, or movement. Each person has his or her own specific health needs. The best way to keep your body healthy is to be conscious about what you eat and drink and do. When you practice being conscious, you will discover your natural ability to know what is good for you.

Perhaps the most important step to good health involves finding the courage to break away from what other people advise: explore and follow those steps that your soul indicates as the best ones for you to take. People who have chosen the path of expanding their consciousness will confirm that once they followed their own path, they did indeed have more energy, health, and joy.

You may have difficulty breaking away from mass thinking because many people in your environment will try to pull you back into their ways of thinking and behaving. Following your path takes courage. However, if you start to live in accordance with your higher self's and soul's messages, you will feel much better.

Learning to live like this takes time because you have to learn to listen to and be sure about what your and soul want for you. You may have changes in some of your relationships. You may lose some, but in the process you will find others that support you.

Realize that the people you yourself may find interesting are probably not the ones who only think and behave according to mass opinion. The people you like or admire the most will be those who follow their own growth path and direction instead of the direction indicated by mass thought forms. Keep in mind that all real progress in science is made by people who have the courage to follow their own creativity and insights, not by people who only think and behave as they "should".

Changing your habits frequently keeps you young and flexible

Consider also the processes of adaptation and habituation. You gain the most consciousness when you give up as many habits as possible. Count your habits; you will be amazed at the number you have. For instance, when you put your trousers on, you usually start with either the left leg or the right. When you wake up and get out of bed, you soon develop a pattern of actions that you keep repeating for a long time. If you keep repeating patterns, you are not really waking up but continuing to sleep a bit. When you have rigid patterns and habits, when your day is built on routine, you do not have to think much about what you are doing. And you will not experience much growth in consciousness.

Think of a vacation during which you discovered all kinds

EARTH CHANGES

of new things and did things much differently than you do them at home. While on vacation, you may have felt much more alive than you feel doing your daily routine at home. The processes of habituation and adaptation are very strong, however. Even when you discover new things, you can easily develop the habit of repeating those things, like always going to the same place on you holiday and always doing the same activities there.

Of course, we are happy that you are coming to Mount Shasta repeatedly. Although you come to the same place every time, you can still try new things and new ways of doing things here. Why not rent skies or snowshoes? On the other hand, do not feel you *must* do new things. When you change or drop habits, accord with the wishes of your inner being.

"Why not rent skies or snowshoes?"

As we come to the end of this chapter, we have one more exercise to put on your list: Do at least one new thing every day, maybe just a small thing. You might buy something you would not usually buy in the supermarket, or visit a shop you have never been in before. What you do doesn't matter; just try something new every day. Breaking your habits will be helpful in expanding your consciousness.

Do you have a question about this?

***

F: Do habits always restrict your consciousness, or can you keep some of the habits you enjoy?

P: Such as...?

F: Such as drinking a cup of coffee and eating Shredded Spoonfuls every morning and enjoying these both.

P: You can keep whatever habits you like. The crucial part is that you really like them. We recommend that you meditate on or think about as many of your habits as possible to find out if they really give you joy. If you are not sure, try to change your habit to experiment. For example, you may quit drinking coffee for a few months and see what benefits you receive. We are not saying you should change everything. Just be observant and conscious of what feels positive in what you are doing. Find out what joy an activity gives you. Do you have any more questions?

F: No.

P: Then this is the end of this chapter. For now, we say good-bye to you with all our love and light.

23.
Meditation: Creating Your Perfect Day

Siskiyou Campground

Welcome, this is Phylos. We greet you from our realms on this mountain and bring you our love and support.

1. Find a comfortable position for your body so that you can relax. While you relax your muscles, feel that your consciousness is expanding, as if you are becoming more aware of your surroundings. Hear the sounds around you, and feel the space around you. Receive the energies that we are transmitting to you and the energies that are about you.

Readers of this book may even feel the energy that was present while this meditation was recorded. Imagine that you sense the energy of this beautiful place, where night is falling and darkness is descending. Expand more and more. Let your awareness drift away in all directions. With every exhale, relax more.

2. Imagine a turbulent energy originating in the area between your eyebrows where your third eye is. Maybe it is a spiral of energy, maybe just whirling energy. First, it may move slowly and then more quickly. You might feel as if your head is getting bigger. The turbulence is opening up the area behind your eyebrows, and you can feel rays of light coming out through your forehead. Keep your head, neck, and shoulders relaxed.

3. The turbulent energy is changing into a bright light—a beautiful, bright, but soft light between the eyes and the area behind the forehead. Let this light help you focus your attention. Start by thinking for a moment about what you did when you woke up. What habits do you recognize? What did you eat and drink today? What did you do, and how did you do these things? Were you quiet, at peace, and focused?

When you review your day, you may find episodes during which your energy was higher and you experienced more peace, more calmness, more joy. Maybe you had episodes during which your energy contracted. Maybe you felt concerned about something. What were you doing when your energy was higher? When it collapsed? What were your thoughts?

4. Think back to the very beginning of your day. Before you start doing anything, be aware of making the transition from sleeping consciousness into waking consciousness. Visualize yourself waking up refreshed. Envision yourself in a quiet, calm, and joyful state; feel yourself having one of your best days ever. Imagine that, while you get up, you take some time to sense the energies present. You take a few deep breaths, and you take time to stretch or do other exercises. You experience no feeling of hurry whatsoever. You are in a calm, serene state, which is your natural state. If you normally do a sequence of rituals at the beginning of your day, you now choose to do things differently. Perhaps you do some exercises or go for a walk in the outside air. Do whatever you feel drawn to do. Enjoy your day. Greet this beautiful new day on the earth plane. Enjoy the fresh air and the wonders of nature. Feel grateful for the food and the comfort you have around you. Eat something different for breakfast today, and do it with great care and tranquility.

5. In this state of high energy and expanded consciousness,

see yourself in complete peace, calmness, and joy for the rest of the day. You love everything you do and you are loving toward everyone you encounter. Let your compassion stream out to animals, plants, and the whole earth. See in everything the wonder of creation. You have a fresh view, as if you are a child, full of love, full of wonder, full of curiosity.

6. Sense how you feel now that you have rewritten your day in such a high way. Maybe you feel inspired to add your own ideas about how to make your day even higher. Realize that it is possible to create every day in this high way. What you can imagine you can create. So, tomorrow you may create another beautiful day.

7. Come back to the here and now. Be conscious of your body and your breath. Feel your connection with the earth. Feel your weight, feel the gravity. When you come back, take a deep breath in and open your eyes. You will remain conscious of the beauty and the peace here for the rest of this day.

For now, we say good-bye to you with all our love and light.

24.
Meditation: Changing a Habit
Siskiyou Campground

Welcome, this is Phylos. You can use this meditation to change a habit.

1. Begin by sitting in a comfortable position. With every exhale, let go of all tension. Find the peace and calmness within.

2. Think of some habit you would like to change. Let go of all the negative thoughts that you have about this habit. First, think about the benefits of having this habit. What do you get from this habit? How does it help you? What does it give you?

3. Ask your higher self if this habit is in alignment with your soul's path. Imagine that your higher self is present now and that it can give you insight into this. Ask your higher self if this habit still serves some purpose for you. Would you benefit from keeping the habit? From changing it? You may hear an answer from your higher self or receive responses through your felt senses.

4. If you feel that you want to change the habit, think about what positive experiences you might have in your life if you changed the habit. Also, if your habit still serves some purpose, think about what to put in the habit's place. Perhaps you have a habit of connecting and interacting with others in a

superficial way—a way that makes you feel safe but that does not serve you anymore. This way of connecting with others gives you protection, but do you still need it? Maybe you can imagine different ways of connecting and interacting with others. When you see yourself acting in a different ways, what positive changes do you experience?

5. Imagine that you changed or gave up the habit. Look at your experiences during the day after you completed that process. Imagine your experiences of the period following that day. Enjoy how your life is different now. You may feel more aligned with your higher path and your soul's path. You may feel that your consciousness has expanded. You may feel more joy and inspiration. Enjoy these feelings. See yourself engaged in alternate activities instead of in the habit.

6. Since habits are strong, you may have days when you miss the habit even if having it would no longer serve you in any way, or perhaps even harm you. Think about what you will do during those moments when you miss this habit. Perhaps you can do something else that is loving for yourself, or enjoy another pleasant activity. Imagine how you might feel a need for the habit and might want it to come back for a while, but how you now turn your attention away from it. Instead, you find some other activity that brings you joy.

7. Now, feel how your breath may have changed. Perhaps you have a feeling of lightness, of being in an open joyful state.

8. You may need to repeat this process several times depending on how strong the habit is and how difficult it is for you to change it. If, nevertheless, you do not succeed in giving it up or if you return to your old habit after a short while, do not blame yourself. Perhaps the time isn't right yet to let the habit go; perhaps it still serves some purpose. Perhaps you need

to focus more on fulfilling the habit's purpose in an alternative way, one which better supports who you are now.

Slowly, at your own pace, come back now and perhaps stretch a bit. For now I say good-bye to you with all my love and support.

25.
Words of Good-bye

Mount Shasta, higher slopes

Our visit to Mount Shasta was coming to an end. On our last evening we went for a short hike on the mountain to the place where the masters wanted to say good-bye to us.

Welcome, this is Phylos, greeting you from our realms high up on this mountain. We bring you a message of love and support. As you climb here, every step you take gives us the opportunity to transmit more of our knowledge and light to you. In this way, you open up to our light and help spread it throughout the world.

We will talk a bit about Jeroen's concerns.

This morning I had expressed some doubts to Froukje about the material I had been channeling. My fear was that not all of it would be new to the readers.

Not everything I say is new to your earth plane. Everything need not be new. However, some major concepts and visions I transmit may, indeed, be new to you. What is important is the bigger picture.

Most importantly, you should know that your life has a purpose and that there is guidance. You are not just a body consisting of chemical processes working on their own. You are a conscious being. You have created and occupied your body. The world as you perceive it is only a small portion of all there is.

By using your outer and your inner senses, you can reach higher states of consciousness in which you get glimpses of other realities. People find it difficult to use their inner senses because their outer senses are so dominant. People find it difficult to make them less dominant.

More exists in our realms than you can perceive with your inner and outer senses. The closest you come to perceiving more is when you perceive light or energies. You can develop this perception in your lifetime. Some people are able to see these flowing energies. At this time, however, only a few people, who have had a lot of training, can see these energies in the same solid way as you see your daily world. However, seeing energies will become increasingly easy. We already spoke about the power of thoughts and about how thoughts create reality. The greater the number of people who develop their inner senses and grow spiritually, the more easily other people will perceive a bigger picture of the universe.

We want to stress that your life and purpose are on the earth plane. That is why so many of the examples we give in this book are from your daily life. That is also why we use the vantage point of your normal senses from which to give our explanations and exercises—and to begin our meditations, which guide you into higher states of awareness.

As we speak our words, we also transmit energies that assist you in your growth and assist our future readers in their growth. Our words will continue to hold this energy even after you have edited the manuscript. This is possible because in our realms we are not limited to time and space as you are. We already know what will happen with this material in the future that you are most likely to choose. We are in contact with every person who will read this material. Our energy will transmit through our words to each reader. This energy is a supportive energy of pure love and creativity, but not of intent, because that is the part you will have to fill in for yourself and our readers will have to fill in for themselves. We just enrich your potential and their potential.

We suggest that you stop here for a while and feel the energy of the mountain. Look around for a moment, and then close your eyes and become very quiet. Feel the energies that are present. We are giving you extra energy as a good-bye gift—to help you on your journey home, and to ease your journey through the next energy shift.

You may perceive how the trees also send you energy, love, and tranquility. Everything around you is focusing its energy on you. The energy gifts you are now receiving can be received by everyone who takes the time to stop, open, and ask for energy.

We now want to speak a few words to those who will be reading this material: you might also close your eyes for a while and imagine that you are standing in the snow on Mount Shasta and that the sun is setting. With every breath you take, imagine and feel our energies coming to you through time and space. Feel accepting and tranquil, while the forces of the earth transmit to you too. Feel the energy that is coming up from deep inside the mountain.

We now say good-bye to you, Froukje and Jeroen, with love, and gratitude for the work you are doing.

We send blessings from our heart. We hope you will have a pleasant journey home, and, of course, we invite you to come back whenever you both find it suitable. We say good-bye to you now with all our love and deep respect for your beings.

PART 3
Divine Intervention

26.
Why Is There Divine?

Bunny Flats Trail

Five months later, in August, we returned to Mount Shasta.

Welcome, this is Phylos, welcoming you back to this beautiful place of high energy. We greet you from high up on our mountain, reaching out through time and space with a message of love and expansion. As we announced earlier, we will now continue our dictation with this section of the book about Divine Intervention. This chapter discusses the question Why is there Divine?

In the first section of the book, you learned about the universe and about being on the earth. In the second part, we taught you about how to live well on the earth plane. That is, how to live in a way that allows you to benefit as much as possible from the goals your soul has set for you in this lifetime. This third part will address the Divine reasons for things on the earth being the way they are. Let us begin by saying this: we generally cannot answer questions about the purposes of your soul and the purposes of the universe from the level of the mental energy body. And yet, to get information about these topics through to you, we have to work with your mental energy body. This situation raises some difficulties for us.

You cannot understand the Divine from the mental level

Consciousness is always striving toward higher forms. Behind that entire process is the Divine. On the mental level, you may have questions like Why does consciousness always strive toward higher forms? Why is there Divinity? Who created God?

These questions cannot be answered from a mental perspective. The real answer is found in *experiencing* the Divine and learning how to work with it in your life. Although we will talk at a mental level about these things, we will also guide you in meditation to give you an opportunity to experience the Divine directly.

Actually, there is no "why" behind it all. It is just how it is. Just as the Divine created the mental energy body, the Divine also created such questions like these. The personality and the mental energy body are frustrated because questions about the purpose of All There Is cannot be answered. From a higher perspective, however, these are senseless questions, because they come from rational thought processes. The Divine is not a mental matter; you can only know the Divine through direct knowledge.

One of the limitations of the earth environment is that direct knowledge is not easy to obtain. At the same time, one of the challenges of earth plane life *is* to obtain direct knowledge.

Direct knowledge is knowledge that is experienced by all your senses—the inner ones as well as the outer ones. Having direct knowledge is knowing with that part of your being that is always there—that part that is much vaster than the part that you are aware of. This vaster part exists in the familiar dimensions as well as other dimensions. Having direct knowledge is having open communication with the higher aspects of your being and with the Divine beyond.

All you are, all you create, all there is, is part of the Divine, and the Divine oversees all of this. Enlightenment occurs when you are completely aware of the Divine and have access to all direct knowledge.

In your life, you have many glimpses of direct contact with the Divine. Such glimpses are so normal for you that you overlook them. In fact, isn't it a miracle divinity can be so normal that you overlook it completely? Divinity is the easiest thing to grasp, and yet at the same time the most difficult because of its obviousness. Divinity is so obvious that your whole science neglects it. How strange! Because at a deeper level, the Divine, which created the earth plane with all of its possibilities, creates all of your scientific discoveries also. The Divine also creates much more directly than your scientists do. Therefore, your scientists have yet to discover that the Divine exists and how you humans can work with it in the earth plane reality.

To know the Divine, you have to release your fear of losing your grip

To work with the Divine, you must first acknowledge its existence. People have so much fear of the Divine and of God that they create all kinds of systems and structures to handle this fear. In a way, one cannot say much about the Divine, and yet whole religions have been built around concepts of God, with all kinds of rules about how to live in order to deal with the Divine in the world. These rules are, at least in part, the result of fear-based reactions. Direct contact with God is so overwhelming that, if you are not ready for it, your experience of it might leave you feeling that you are losing your grip on the world—which, in fact you are. People often react to fear by creating rules.

Losing your grip on the world is only scary from the perspective of the personality which was created to enable you to live in this world with all its restricting rules. However, the restrictions that you experience on the earth plane do not exist at the higher levels of your real, multidimensional self. There your consciousness is free-floating. People are so afraid of losing their grip on the world that they create many ways to make this grip even stronger.

Consider all the man-made rules that you humans have imposed upon your world. For example, before you could start this walk today, you had to complete a lot of man-made paperwork to obtain a wilderness permit so you could enter this park. Also man-made are the tools you use for eating and the rules for handling them. All these man-made phenomena serve the purpose of helping you keep your grip on life. We could give you many more examples of how man-made rules impact your daily life. If you were to record everything you do in a day that results from man-made rules, you would be amazed. Saying Good morning or Good-bye, closing doors, or walking on the pavement instead of the grass border, are just a few examples.

Persons who are very rigid or have obsessive-compulsive disorders are so afraid of losing their grip that they impose even more rules upon themselves. The solution to their problems lies in re-establishing their contact with Divinity. This solution may work better than your contemporary psychiatry—which is also composed of man-made rules—works.

Humans have also invented most thought systems, the

purpose of which is to help the personality keep a grip on life. To explain these matters to you, we have to work with rules and systems like your language. We have to do this because there is no other way to make things clear to you—besides direct experience of the Divine. Our meditations may help you to experience some of that.

You may take a break now.

After a short break during which we discussed what Phylos had just said, we started walking again and Phylos continued the dictation.

As Froukje said during the break, rules also simplify daily life. That, of course, is true, and yet on another level these rules govern your thinking so powerfully that they limit your view of the world and blur your direct contact with the Divine. You will benefit by becoming more conscious about what purpose rules serve. Some serve a higher purpose such as creating an easy flow of life. Others serve the personality's purpose of keeping a grip on the world because the personality is afraid of losing control of its life.

To know the Divine, find beauty and love in everything

The Divine is always so obviously present behind everything in your world that you hardly notice it. The main qualities of the Divine are beauty and love. As you concentrate on the beauty of whatever you perceive, you perceive the Divine behind it. As you concentrate on the love you feel for whatever form, living or not, you perceive the Divine behind that form.

Some scientists maintain that the ability to perceive

beauty and love are survival mechanisms, which the human race has evolved. I tell you they are not. Beauty and love are a manifestation of Divine Energy permeating everything inside and outside you and your world. Beauty and love do not have a physical form. Words cannot explain what beauty or love is. When you listen to scientific explanations of these qualities, you will see that the essence of the qualities is missing from the explanations. You cannot describe the experience of these qualities in words. As a rule of thumb, you might say that you are perceiving the Divine when you cannot put a beautiful experience into words.

This is the end of this chapter. For now, we say good-bye you with all our love and light.

27.
Meditation: Finding Divine Energy
Bunny Flats

Welcome, this is Phylos, greeting you with a message of love and support from up high on our mountain.

1. We invite you to find a comfortable sitting position and connect with the silence within you. Find your place of inner silence, the silence that is behind thoughts and emotions. As you bring more and more of your attention into that silence, you might notice that this place of silence is a place of observation. In this silent place, which is the core of your being at the transition point between the dimensions of your earth realm and the dimensions of other realms, you can more easily perceive yourself as energy.

2. Find your thoughts now as energy. You might ask yourself what a thought is. Observe some of your thoughts. Look at them. What are they but energies? Next, remaining in that place of silence, look at your emotions and feelings. What are feelings but energies? Also observe your physical body and the sensations you feel in your physical body. What are they but energies?

When you perceive from your inner place of silence, you perceive only energy. As you sit with your eyes closed, you might even ask yourself where your physical body is right now.

The only thing you perceive now is sensations. Sensations are just energy. From that place of inner silence, look out now with your inner eye at the energies that you perceive as being you.

3. Find the energy that underlies all the energies that you perceive in your emotional and mental flow. Find a frequency or a set of base frequencies that you perceive in each one of your energy systems. That common frequency is your essence, or your base tone.

4. Open yourself to the light and to the rays of the sun. As you do, you may perceive that these rays contain the energy of the soul of the sun, pure life-force energy. See or feel how this life-force energy forms all the energetic and physical structures upon the basic energy that is you.

5. Find the energy that underlies all this, and open your energy even more. Some part of you knows how to do this. Open your shoulder blades as though you are creating more space in that area of your body. Also, open the top of your head more, so you can feel or see the Divine Energy. How do you perceive the qualities of this energy with its high, pure light, which contains the frequencies of love, purpose, and beauty? Let these frequencies come into your energy field now. Find them there as a constant flow of supportive energy.

6. You might realize that without this Divine Energy, energies would float aimlessly and without direction. See how the Divine Light gives direction to the life force energy of the soul of the sun, and to your own energy. Also, feel how the life force energy of the soul of the sun is part of your own energy. Without this energy you would not be.

7. You may stay in this energy as long as you wish, and, when you are ready, come back in your own way and at your own pace.

For now, we say good-bye to you with all our love and light.

28.
The Divine Is in Everything
Bunny Flats

Welcome, this is Phylos, greeting you from our realms high up on the mountain. Perhaps you have felt some physical and mental discomfort lately. We have been working with your energies to increase your ability to receive our transmissions of light and information, and to ease your contact with my dear brother, St. Germain. He is with us all the time, primarily to take care of Froukje's energy. What you two are doing here takes a lot of openness, willingness, and concentration, and we acknowledge you for having come far enough to be able to help us deliver these materials.

Before we start with today's chapter, we want to comment on your experience in the cafe this morning with the man who wanted a cup of coffee.

Before our walk at Bunny Flats today, we had a wonderful soup and salad in the nice local cafe called Bagels Cafe. A man came into the cafe. When the waitress refused to give him a cup of coffee because he had no money, he became very angry. Things happened very quickly, and when he left, Froukje regretted our not buying him a coffee. Soon, however, he returned with some money. Although it was not enough to pay for a coffee, the waitress gave him a cup. When he left, he had a nice, soft look in his eyes and gave Froukje a big smile. Froukje assumed that the episode was a lesson in sharing for us from the masters, and that we had missed it.

The man did not have money to pay for the coffee, and he was angry. Do not worry that you did not buy him the coffee. Froukje's intuition was right—behind his angry energy was a divine lesson for both of you. Although he is a human being, we sent him to you for this lesson in divinity. We compliment you, Froukje, for recognizing the divinity in him even though you did not follow your impulse to buy him a cup of coffee. Afterward, you recognized this had been a lesson about sharing, so you learned what you had to learn anyhow. Now we will continue with the chapter.

The theme of today's chapter is that the Divine is in everything. This, in fact, sums up the chapter's content. Nevertheless, we will elaborate a bit on this subject. As we explained in our last chapter, while the Divine is very close to you, it is also very removed from you because of all the illusions that operate upon the earth plane. These prevent you from seeing the Divine clearly and experiencing it directly.

You can learn to perceive the Divine Light directly

Since everything is divine, humanity's most important goal is to re-establish contact with the Divine. Our main reason for delivering our information over and over again is to help humanity remember its Divine Source. Making that connection is humanity's highest purpose and greatest learning experience. The information we give you is always adapted to humanity's level of development at the moment of giving.

The time has come for humanity to experience the Divine

in more direct ways. At the personality level as well as at the soul level, an open connection with divinity brings great happiness into the lives of humans. When people realize that everything is divine, they develop deep joy and caring, and deep respect for everything. The time has come for you to open your eyes. Every time you see beauty or feel love, you are in contact with the Divine. You might focus more of your life upon seeing and finding beauty and love.

When you are depressed, you may feel a lack of beauty and love; you may even feel that beauty and love are not available to you. This, however, is an illusion. If you feel depressed, know that an enormous amount of love is available to you. All you need to do is open to this love so that you can find beauty, love, and joy again. The Divine is love, and since you are divine, you yourself are love, and there is plenty of Divine Love for you. We ascended masters, angelic beings, and guides are sending you love even if you feel that you cannot receive it.

When you lift the veils of illusion, you can perceive the Divine directly. Although you cannot perceive the Divine Light with your normal senses, we can tell you about it by describing it as though it were visible light.

If you can perceive the Divine Light in your world directly, you may see it as a fluid, whitish light pouring down on everything. You might visualize it as something between a fluid and a gas. The light pours over and into everything in your world. For example, the trees are covered with a white shine, which moves somewhat like liquid gas moves. Just try to imagine this light, even if you cannot perceive it directly. Your imagination will help you get closer to an experience of direct perception of this light.

You may also see how this light enlivens everything it touches. It causes the beautiful patterns underlying all life forms, including those of the mineral kingdom, to radiate. The Divine Light illuminates and activates their underlying patterns. What you perceive with your daily consciousness and senses are the forms, colors, and patterns that result from this illumination of basic patterns. Think of a computer. Although no current may be flowing through it, many kinds of imperceptible structures and patterns exist within it. When you switch it on, you can perceive a great variety of forms and colors on the screen.

With your normal senses, you cannot perceive the patterns that underlie every form on the earth. But when you perceive the Divine Light directly, you also perceive the structures and patterns that underlie everything. You perceive how that fluid white light illuminates these beautiful structures.

Imagine that your body consists of all kinds of underlying independent structures interacting with each other. The Divine Light illuminates them, so you can see that you are not just a body—that you are alive, you have consciousness, and you can perceive the world.

We recommend that you imagine this when you meditate so that you can actually experience more of it. When you open to the beauty and love of All There Is, you will experience a deep feeling of connection, gratitude, and bliss. This feeling starts with a sense of peace and quiet which you perceive in your chest. Sometimes this feeling also triggers old patterns in your auras. The patterns that are triggered may cause temporary emotional imbalance or physical discomfort. For example, Froukje, who is very open to the direct flow of Divine Energy, at times experiences physical discomfort and emotional unbalance.

Letting the Divine come into your life will bring you happiness and joy, a feeling of connection with everything, and a deep caring for everything. People who have this experience will find that they no longer have any reasons to fight, and, indeed, they will start sharing part of their money or possessions. The consequences will be enormous. For example, the whole monetary system will disappear and the way the economy works will change drastically. You need courage to open to the Divine because doing so can bring up basic survival issues. The rewards, however, are tremendous.

Experiencing the Divine Light is better than speaking about it. We will guide you to a special place of power and lead you into a meditation there.

29.
Meditation: Revitalizing in the Divine Light
Bunny Flat, Forgiveness Stone

Welcome, this is Phylos. Today we have brought you to this special place of high energy. During the first half of the twentieth century, we appeared in places like this one. As you concentrate, you may feel our energies here—almost as a physical presence.

1. Imagine you are sitting in a high energy place that holds the quality of forgiveness. That place may be at home in a chair or wherever you are. Just imagine that the place in which you are sitting is one in which you receive forgiveness and forgive others easily. As you sit with your eyes closed, relax, become quiet inside, and feel the stream of forgiveness. Feel the quality of unconditional love that is in this energy of forgiveness.

If you have difficulty feeling this, let that be all right. Just imagine that you can feel what the quality of forgiveness is like. You may experience a soft feeling in your chest, quietness, or an emotion, maybe sadness.

2. If tears come, they may be a mixture of deep emotions such as sorrow, gratitude, love, and beauty. The soft energies of forgiveness stream through you. Forgiveness streams into your physical, etheric, emotional, and mental bodies. Whether you perceive it or not, feel or imagine this soft stream of light, and recognize that it comes from a divine source.

3. Recognize that although the Divine is present in everything, a special and deep love and forgiveness is present for you personally. As you concentrate on this love and forgiveness, even more of it becomes available. Do so now, or ask for Divine Love and be open to receive it. Feel the potential of this love and its soft stream of forgiveness.

4. Imagine that all the cells of your body are opening to receive this light. Notice how a beautiful shimmer of light emerges from them. See a sparkling, white, fluid light pouring through every cell of your body. Feel how this light stimulates every cell. Every cell has a consciousness of its own; every cell experiences joy and gratitude. Your cells and organs light up with gratitude and love. Radiant health pours through your body because this Divine Light is the most healing energy that exists. It is a light of pure potential, potential for whatever is needed, be it healing, love, or support.

5. Imagine now that the white, fluid, Divine Light is pouring all over your body. Perhaps you can feel it on your skin as a soft touch. See or imagine how you yourself begin to radiate more light. Places in your body that need healing are lighting up too, starting to get healthier. Imagine that this light emanates from your entire being, as though you are in a clear cloud of light.

6. In this light, beings of light, angels and guides appear. You are doing fine, even if you do not see anything. Just let your experience unfold regardless of what you are seeing. You may experience these beings as entities, or light in a sea of love, or you may have a feeling of connection. Feel how you are loved, and send your love and gratitude to these angelic messengers of God in return.

7. Know that every moment you spend concentrating on these beings and asking for light, you receive it. You grow

spiritually when you open yourself to this light, whether the light comes directly from the Divine or by means of messengers of light. You also help humanity attain a higher level of consciousness and open more to the Divine.

8. Now, at your own pace, gently come back. When you are back, take some time to feel what this light has done for you.

We now say good-bye with our deepest love and respect for your being.

30.
Levels of Growth

Bunny Flats to Panther Meadows

Upper Panther Meadow: Saint Germain's Spring

Welcome, this is Phylos. From our realms up on high on this beautiful mountain, we send our love and energy to you and through you to humanity. Today's chapter is about levels of growth.

When you think in terms of systems and hierarchies, you create them

When we speak about levels and hierarchies, we are

simplifying the true multidimensional nature of reality. Levels and hierarchies are constructions of the mental energy body. Nevertheless, we will use these divisions for teaching purposes.

Humanity in its present phase of growth has a fairly well-developed mental energy body. Since the mind is structured to think in systems, levels, and hierarchies, it is eager to hear about them. The truth is that the universe is not as hierarchical as the mental body believes. Actually, the universe is multidimensional, and many of its aspects are beyond what your mental energy body can understand. We have to simplify and translate these aspects into your language for you to be able to understand some of them.

When people work with astrology or psychology, they may believe that these systems represent the truth about reality because these subjects can be systemized. However, this is not the case. Systems are superficial ways of describing multidimensional aspects of energy. Astrology is correct in stating that star energies influence your life, but people often interpret the system of astrology far too literally. Star energies work in a highly individual way as they interact with the individual, the energies present on the earth, and the particular way the Divine Energy is working at a given moment.

Furthermore, thoughts create reality, so by developing systems you create these systems in your reality. Then you see them work, and you say that the system is real because it works. Psychiatry, for example, thinks in systems that, in fact, create psychiatric disorders. When the systems change, the problems change. Multiple personality disorder is now quite a common diagnosis, while some years ago it did not exist, or existed only in a marginal way. In addition, hysteria, once a popular diagnosis, is not that prominent anymore. Believers in older systems will deny that there is such a thing as the very existence of multiple personality disorder, saying that it cannot have come into being out of nothing. The truth is that since there are more and more who believe in this disorder, it has gradually been created whereas some older diagnoses have disappeared along with the disorders themselves.

This truth applies to all systems of thought, including many religious texts. You may be interested to know that this also applies to the idea that channeling is possible. This idea created the reality which is evident now.

Humanity moves through levels of growth with distinct transitions

We now come to the main topic of this chapter: levels of growth.

When you observe the human condition on earth, you can identify levels of development which humans go through in one or more lifetimes. When enough individuals attain a certain level of growth, humanity as a whole moves on to the next level.

The way humanity grows might be compared to the way the seed of a plant opens and grows. The plant's mature form is determined by the seed and by the circumstances. On an energy level, the seed is the life force energy and the consciousness incarnated in the individual. The circumstances are the energies present on the earth, the creations of mass thinking, and the Divine Energy and Divine Intervention.

We will talk now about the stages of growth of the individual. People move through distinct stages of growth. You go through specific transitions as you move from one stage to the next. However, reality is more complicated than this. Your personality and your soul have many aspects and many dimensions, so it is possible that different parts of you are working on different levels of growth simultaneously.

The first stages are literally about survival. Before birth, a body has to be formed. It must be stable in form and have auras that enable it to exist in the earth dimensions. Creating this body is a great accomplishment of life force energy. The sources of this energy are the soul of your sun, the Divine, and the will of the conscious being that wants to incarnate in that body. The soul incarnates in the fetus, either directly after conception or later in the pregnancy. After birth, gradually the personality takes over as the journey on the earth plane begins.

After the wonder of conception and birth, comes the *first level* of growth, the level of survival. On this level, humans use all their consciousness to provide for things like food, shelter, and safety.

On the *second level* of growth, the personality develops personal wishes. At the lower levels, these wishes are often for material things, or are based on the body's desires and pleasures. These wishes are partly goals of the physical body, which has its own consciousness. Although the soul too may have set some goals at these lower levels, its goals mostly develop during later stages of the person's development. People who are trapped in this second level will be interested mostly in material things or in bodily pleasures such as sexuality, food, and drink.

On the *third level*, more soul consciousness is involved, and the individual begins to be interested in personal growth, but still in quite an egotistical form. The personality may be interested in evolving and having higher experiences by, for example, enjoying art, or pursuing therapies for personal growth.

Spirituality starts on the third and the fourth levels. Many people in spiritual movements are on the third and forth levels. People who are on the third level may become interested in spirituality, but from an egotistical perspective, where their personality gains are still central. They may move on to higher levels if the Divine taps them on the shoulder, so to speak.

Many people are now on the *fourth level.* Here they hope for a higher life, and begin to love and care for their surroundings. Their spirituality is awakened and they develop a real caring for others. Their love for others and for nature increases. Qualities like harmony, order, and respect evolve. Many people on this level do bodywork, for example, or explore different kinds of therapies. While these activities in themselves are not spiritual, they may be important for personal growth.

Although working on personal growth is good for your personal development and prepares you for the next level of growth, reaching directly for the next levels is better and more effective. Meditation, for example, is a strong and direct way to reach for the spiritual levels directly.

To develop beyond the fourth level, you need to develop an unconditional love for humanity and for nature. It is important to ask yourself whether your love is sincere. If you have a hidden motive for loving—if you hope to receive love in return for your love—you will need to learn to love yourself more before you will be able to move on to the next level. True unconditional love is part of the next stage.

Real spirituality begins on the *fifth level.* Here you work with soul energy and soul qualities. The individual develops soul qualities like love, respect, beauty, clarity, and so on. True unconditional love for the environment, for other people, and for nature develops. Materialistic goals become less important, and spiritual growth is the main focus. Many people, who had egotistical motivations when they first began taking courses in spiritual growth, move on to these higher levels.

On the *sixth level,* the realization that the Divine influences everything evolves from the mental and emotional level to the intuitive level of direct knowledge. Although the Divine is present on every level and in everything, at the sixth level the Divine enters your being in profound ways and you become conscious of your awakening.

Your intuitive energy body develops quite easily on this level. You experience direct knowledge of the Divine and have a strong wish for a constant, conscious contact with it. On this level of growth, you can reach states of consciousness that are sometimes called peak experiences or states of bliss.

On the *seventh level*, your senses lose their veils and you can perceive the Divine Light directly. On these higher levels, you are becoming a realized person. Gurus are at these levels.

Of all the beings that are incarnated on the earth plane, avatars are at the highest levels, closest to the Divine. In the spiritual realm, angels, guides, masters, and other beings of light exist at these levels.

All these levels of growth exist simultaneously. You cannot say you are on one specific level only. Mostly you are on more than one level at once. Only truly realized beings and avatars exist exclusively at the higher levels, although even these are also bound to the lower levels in some ways.

Do not blame other people for living their lives mainly on the lower levels. There is nothing wrong with existing mainly on the lower levels. The levels on which you and your soul are working depend on where you can learn the most for the development of the soul. You might be working primarily on the lower levels in this lifetime, while your soul is working on a higher level in another lifetime simultaneously. Most important is that you strive towards developing yourself in a joyful way, regardless of your level.

Humanity is on the verge of shifting to the fifth level

The levels of growth that apply to the individual also apply to humanity as a whole. At this time, humanity is making a shift from the fourth to the fifth level. The intuitive energy body is developing in order to ease this process. The more people who commit to their growth on whatever level, the more easily humanity as a whole will shift to the next level. A great part of humanity is mainly on the second or third level now. People who are interested in the growth movement and who are working on their personal growth are mainly on the third and fourth level. Maybe some are on the fifth.

Fortunately, not all people have to be at these higher levels in order to create a change for humanity as a whole. A group of people working on the higher levels greatly affects the development of consciousness for humanity as a whole. In fact, their impact in *raising* the consciousness of humanity is about five times greater than the impact a group of people on a lower level has on *lowering* the consciousness of humanity. If all people were on the fourth level and a group of them were to move back to the third level, the impact on the growth of humanity would be minimal. The reason for this difference in impact is that consciousness is always striving toward higher forms. Once a new possibility is achieved, it will not be dismissed easily.

This is the end of this chapter. We say good-bye to you for now with all our love and light.

***

P: Now, Froukje, you had some questions.

F: Can we become realized during our lives, or will we stay on our present level?

P: As we said, even avatars still function partly on the lower levels too. If you function only on the higher levels, you may lose contact with earth reality and with the earth itself. In earth life, you must stay in touch with the earth dimension with all its restrictions. While you are in a period between lives, you are actually realized.

It is possible to become realized in one lifetime. However, very few people exist on the higher levels with as much as eighty percent of their consciousness. Usually the people who become realized in one lifetime have about sixty percent of their energy in these higher dimensions and forty percent in the earth dimension. However, some avatars are in the higher dimensions with more than eighty percent of their consciousness right from the start.

F: Like Mother Meera?

P: Indeed, like Mother Meera or Sai Baba.

If your question is about yourself, the answer is yes, you can become realized in this lifetime, but whether or not you will actually do it depends on your choices. As we see your lives unfolding, we observe that you both have a strong attachment to the earth dimension, so we think you will most probably stay in the earth dimension with most of your consciousness. You may be at the third, fourth, and fifth levels, and experience glimpses of the sixth and maybe the seventh.

F: When you look at the choices we are making, would you say that we will stay connected to the earth?

P: Yes. Again, the point is this: being at higher or lower levels is neither good nor bad. Your personality may feel that you should go as high as possible, but your most appropriate level is mainly a matter of what your soul wants for you in this lifetime. What is most important is to follow what gives you the most joy and love, and to receive your soul's messages. Perhaps your soul wants you to go to the seventh level or higher, but it may well choose to have lessons at the lower levels in this lifetime. Do not focus on going as high as possible, just find what gives you the most joy. Going high may give you joy, but so does life on the earth plane. Do not get stuck in the belief that going higher is always better.

F: I know you will not tell me what our goals are from our soul's perspective. But I want to ask you what our souls want for us in this lifetime. Or is this something that cannot be revealed?

P: We might wonder if your soul itself knows what it wants for you in this lifetime. The soul is quite an abstract form of consciousness. Compared to the higher forms of Divine Energy however, it is less abstract. Your soul has a more clearly defined purpose and will. Your soul also has a stronger sense of identity. You, the individual, have a lot of freedom to fulfill this purpose or to create forms of your own.

On an abstract level, we do know what your soul's purpose in this lifetime is. But putting that into words is not easy. You are right in saying that we are reluctant to reveal your soul's purpose. Your purpose is, for the most part, something you should discover by yourself. Life purpose has many aspects to it. If we would state your life purpose in words, you might not see the flexible, multidimensional aspects of life purpose. Furthermore, you might think, This is it, and stop exploring more possibilities and challenges that life has for you.

F: Can the soul change its purpose during a lifetime because the personality makes other choices?

P: When we discuss the concept of life purpose, you may think that your soul has only one purpose for you in this lifetime. However, your soul's purposes are both numerous and multidimensional. In fact, purpose is an *energy* that changes from moment to moment for you and for your soul. Yet at the same time, a characteristic of purpose is that it has a strong direction.

As you lift the veils of illusion of your perception, you will recognize that the continuity of your earth plane being is an illusion too. This illusion is created by the mechanisms of adaptation and habituation, and by the mechanisms of the mind, which makes predictions about the world in order to maintain the idea of the constancy of the world.

You might realize that, on the personality level just as on the soul level, purpose is a fluctuating matter. However, each lifetime has an outline. If the personality decides not to follow that outline, the soul will usually not change its purpose, because the outline was set for specific reasons and learning experiences. When people lose contact with their soul-destination, their lives may end sooner, or their lives will become more of a struggle. The soul does not intend to punish a person who is not following his or her higher path. This is just how the energy of the universe works. Following the flow is a lot easier than going against it, just like paddling a boat downstream is a lot easier than paddling it upstream.

F: Is this related to what you talked about before, namely that a person who loses contact with his or her soul can become mentally confused?

P: That is indeed possible, although a person can also get mentally confused because that is his or her soul's purpose. However, in the latter case there will be great learning opportunities. Only mass thinking sees confusion as an undesirable state.

F: I have a question about the earlier part of the chapter

relating to how your thoughts influence your reality. Is it true that when people stop thinking that multiple personality disorder exists, it will disappear?

P: That is true.

F: And will those people who have the disorder now have another disorder instead, or will they be healthy?

P: That depends on the person's reason for having the disorder and on the person's beliefs. You can only have a multiple personality disorder if public opinion acknowledges this condition. In earlier centuries, some persons had this condition, but no one else recognized that they had it and they themselves did not recognize the condition because it did not exist in mass thinking. When the mass thinking changes, the disorder will disappear. Probably you will see a different disorder emerge, one in accordance with the new mass thinking. So if hysteria were to come back into mass thinking, these persons might become hysterical.

F: And what will happen when we all stop thinking about psychiatric illnesses and when we all start believing that everybody has a healthy mind?

P: In some cultures on the earth, people do not think in terms of psychiatric illness. In those cultures, such illnesses do not exist. People with psychoses, as defined by your culture, may be well-respected medicine men in another culture—and you cannot say they are psychotic because they are not. They would only begin to be psychotic if they were transferred into western society.

F: I have another question. If you raise your child with love and warmth, will the child be able to contact its soul earlier and skip a few levels?

P: When a child is born, it has chosen the conditions of its birth. If it is born in a safe western country, its start in life is easier than if it is born in a war zone. If the parents educate the child well, giving love and attention to the child's spiritual aspects, it can grow through these levels faster. However, most important is teaching your children to be free to learn their own lessons. Avoid imposing systems upon your children. We realize that this is almost impossible for parents since they raise their children within the context of their parental belief system. However, we suggest that you not pressure your children to believe what you believe. You can give your children your education but we suggest that you also give them many opportunities to experience all kinds of spiritual streams and directions of thought. This would be better than imposing your own spirituality. Does this answer the question?

F: Yes, thank you very much.

P: Did you have any more questions?

F: No, that is all.

P: Then we will stop here for now. We thank you for your questions that help to clarify these materials. Good-bye.

31.
Meditation: Entering the Higher Dimensions of Your Being

Dead Fall Meadow

Welcome this is Phylos. We greet you from up on our mountain, reaching out to you through time and space with our messages of love and support.

1. First, tune in to your own energy. Draw your attention into the very core of your being, that point of observation behind your thoughts, emotions, and sensations. To find this place, observe your thoughts and notice the stillness between them. Find that place of inner stillness, the peace that is there, and the easy contact with love and beauty.

2. As you stay in that place of inner stillness, imagine that you are in a beautiful place, a place of power. Sense the energies of an increasingly wider area around you. Use your inner senses to contact these energies and to find other dimensions of your being.

3. Visualize your normal reality as a kind of a cone with the apex pointing upward. On top of that cone is a much larger cone and its apex points downward. In this larger cone, your being exists in the other dimensions. Move your awareness up through the precise point where the two apexes meet, so that you enter this other-dimensional part of your being. Play for a while with focusing your attention in these other dimensions, finding them at more and more levels.

4. Imagine or feel that you are in other dimensions of your being now, and experience the vastness of your being. You may discover layer upon layer, dimension upon dimension. You may move back and forth between the cones a few times, moving from the lower cone into the inverted upper cone, from the daily reality to the other dimensions of yourself. Stop awhile at the point between them, which is the transition point between the dimensions. This point is a doorway, an entrance point, at which you can shift your attention from your daily reality to the higher aspects and other dimensions of your being. At this point, the light of the higher dimensions enters your being.

While moving up and down through this point, you will feel more and more light building around you, emerging precisely from this transition point.

5. While keeping your awareness at the transition point, notice the light building more and more. Feel that you are in a vast space, a place of much light indeed. Just let this light carry you for a while. At this transition point, which is both very small and very vast, you can easily experience divine energies. Feel the energies of purpose and love here. You may experience them as specific vibrations.

6. Take some time to find, more precisely, this divine vibration of purpose and love within the sea of energies. This vibration is a soft light, which carries you and nourishes you. Although this light is so obviously present, it normally goes unnoticed. This underlying soft stream of Divine Love and purpose is carrying you, and is literally feeding you. All life forms are created and nourished by this energy.

If you lose contact with this energy, play again with going up and down between your normal reality and the other aspects of your self. Move through the cones and find the transition point again. A sudden increase in the light you experience may tell you that you have found this transition point with your awareness. The precise location of the transition point is not important. Just let your experience be the right one for you.

7. Now feel in this light the quality of purpose in its purest form, both as an energy and as a driving force. Find its qualities in their purest form. You may feel some of the divine driving force that lies behind this energy. At the same time, it is a very gentle, nonintrusive energy.

8. You are within a vast light. Now imagine how all the energy flows from this light flow through the transition point and focus into your soul and your earth being.

9. Think about something you wish to manifest or a question you may have about your life purpose. Find this wish or question as energy now, and see how pure energy from the higher dimensions comes through this transition point into the energy of your wish or question. Feel the soft energy of purpose as it permeates the energy of your wish or question. You may see this energy as colors or patterns that may be moving around.

10. Now leave the transition point between the dimensions, and move back to your place of inner silence. Connect with the energies of your environment again, and feel your connection to that environment.

11. Whether or not your received an answer to your question is not important. In this meditation we have connected with the pure Divine Energy of purpose and focused it into your soul and your personality. The results of this will unfold easily; we have sown the seed of an inner knowing so that you can more easily follow your intuition and your path.

Realize that any decisions you need to make to follow the path of your soul should not be made on the mental plane but on the intuitive plane. If you use your intuitive energy body to help you make decisions, things will work our better for you.

12. Come back now at your own pace. We say good-bye to you with our deepest love and with deep respect for the beings that you are.

32.
Divine Intervention

Mount Shasta Lower Slopes

Welcome, this is Phylos, joyful to connect with you so many times. Today's chapter discusses Divine Intervention.

The greatest force operating on the earth plane is the Divine Force. Every life and every structure is created from the Divine Light. To help humanity find its path of truth, we, ascended masters, help bring this light down in its pure energy form, and also in the form of knowledge—as in these teachings. Humanity has only one destination, and that destination is reunion with the Divine. The Divine creates and inspires all actions—ranging from the simplest actions, for example, those within the smallest atoms, to the most complex actions. Yet every spark of consciousness also has freedom of action in itself.

There is a divine plan behind everything that happens

The natural goal of everything in the universe is to strive toward greater perfection, greater love, and higher forms. The question Why is this so? is extremely difficult to answer. It is just the way the universe is. You can only *experience* the Divine.

You may experience divine sparks when you feel happy and joyous, or when you see beautiful forms—perhaps when you enjoy the beauty of art, or when you feel fulfilled by your actions, or even when you enjoy seeing a machine that is functioning smoothly. The answer to the question Why? is not a mental one. The answer is an experience of beauty, order, fulfillment, and joy of Divine Perfection.

Every person has his or her own consciousness, and because of that has free will. This free will can be used in different ways, which are influenced by that person's level of growth. The Divine always offers guidance, either directly or through angels, masters, guides, and other beings of light. The higher the level of the light being, the more abstract its guidance may be.

When we speak of Divine Intervention, we speak of qualities like love and beauty. Different religions stress different aspects of the Divine. Some religions emphasize the quality of order. Too much emphasis on order may result in too many rules and thus rigidity. Other religions emphasize love. Too much emphasis on love, and only love, can result in people neglecting their worldly tasks. All the main religions acknowledge one Divine Force behind the reality that you perceive. Their essence is the same. Their differences are far less important than their shared acknowledgment of an underlying Divine Oneness.

We prefer to talk about the Divine as possessing the qualities of love, creativity, and intent. Other qualities like clarity, order, and so on, which are derived from the Divine, might be called soul qualities. All of these qualities are what you might, in earth terms, call positive qualities.

Negative qualities, or evil, also exist, but only because your world is constructed with divisions. Divisions create opposites. Good creates bad. However, when you transcend the restrictions that operate upon the earth plane, only pure energies exist. Energies in their pure form are only positive or good, although in truth, these qualities are neither negative nor positive. They just are the way they are.

The Divine is subtle and yet full of power

The Divine Force operating on the earth plane is very subtle and at the same time omnipotent. This seeming contradiction has to do with your perceptual mechanisms. If your consciousness is not yet open enough, you will not perceive much of the Divine that is everywhere and in everything. It is so obvious that it is easily overlooked.

We might use the analogy of the fish in its fishbowl again. The fish does not recognize that it is in water because that fact is so obvious. As the fish encounters different temperatures of water, its body will adapt to these and hardly notice them. Divine Intervention on the earth plane operates in a similar way. As you encounter many different "temperatures," you undergo subtle, yet powerful changes. You may hardly notice the different rays of Divine Energy that operate upon the earth, giving direction to the development of all life on earth.

At this time, an important shift in the energy on the earth plane is occurring. Divine Intervention has initiated the development of the intuitive energy body. This energy body enables you to have more direct contact with the divine qualities of love, creativity, and intent, which are the basic components of earth-consciousness. The development of this energy body will also make it easier for you to perceive the Divine.

However, the intuitive energy body, as well as your other

energy bodies and your physical body, may function more or less effectively, depending on whether or not you activate or neglect its possibilities. One of the purposes of our lesson today is to prevent you from buying a beautiful new car, so to speak, just to keep it in the garage all of its life. Our purpose is to help you recognize that the beautiful machine in your garage can be used and driven.

We have talked before about how you can recognize Divine Energy. Meditation and other techniques can help connect you to the Divine. Realize that the Divine is loving, and that the direction it gives to humanity as a whole, and to every single person, is one of greater evolution and more happiness.

This is the end of this chapter. For now, we say good-bye to you with all our love and light.

33.
Meditation: Entering Other Dimensions
Mount Shasta KOA Campground

Welcome, this is Phylos, greeting you from up on high with a message of love and support.

1. As you sit now with eyes closed, make contact with your inner being. How does your body feel? Is there any tension? How are your emotions right now? How are your thoughts right now? How is your connection with the higher realms? With every breath you take, enhance your awareness of your observations of these sensations and feelings. Feel yourself at peace.

2. Now use your inner senses to connect with your surroundings. If you are sitting on a chair, feel its solidity and connection with the earth. Also feel your own connection with the earth.

3. Expand your awareness from the place where you are sitting to a greater area around you. Notice that you can quite easily sense the area around you.

4. Then go back to your own energy. Retreat more and more into your inner being, letting all the outside influences, such as noises, become increasingly distant. Just let them go. Retreat more and more to the place of inner stillness that is behind your thoughts, feelings, and sensations. One way to find this place is to observe your thoughts and the silence between them.

Notice the stillness between your thoughts. Notice the inner silence and pure awareness which precede the emergence of a new thought. This space of inner silence exists behind your thoughts, emotions, and bodily sensations. From this place, you may easily observe your thoughts, feelings, and sensations. Bring all your awareness to this place. You might find this place as a smaller and smaller area of light in the very core of your being. Where in your body you perceive this place may change. It might be somewhere in your upper spine, where your back becomes your neck. Or it might be in your chest. The precise location is not that important. Notice the peace, the nothingness, yet also the fullness.

5. Now bring even more of your awareness into this silent place, and go right into it, as though you are moving through a doorway into a vast space that seems to stretch out behind you. This doorway leads you to other dimensions and other worlds. Observe the place you are entering now. Perceive the vastness of that world as you pass the place of inner silence. Notice that you can move into this space while still knowing that your body is somewhere behind you. You may even turn around and look at your body as it sits, waiting patiently while you explore these spaces.

6. Notice the quality of this space, and how it is that you move through it. Notice whether this energy has a certain texture. When you move into this space the first time, do not move into it too far. Just look around and notice more and more of the richness here. You may or may not perceive structures, forms, and perhaps beings that are here. On some level, you may still be conscious of your physical body all the time.

Notice the quality of the energies that are present. Many energies and vibrations that you might use are here. Many are new for you, so take time to select suitable vibrations for you. Notice for example a purifying light that comes in waves.

7. After exploring this vast world for a while, you may return to the doorway. Just thinking about this doorway brings you back there. Move back through it so you come back into your place of inner silence. Again, notice the light and the peace here.

8. Now slowly, at your own pace, come back to your daily consciousness as we say good-bye to you now with all our love and light.

34.
Being a Focus of Light for Everyone
Sky Bowl to Squaw Meadows

Welcome this is Phylos. This chapter discusses how to be a focus of light for everyone. You can choose a path of development that makes it easier to change yourself so that you can live in greater alignment with the purposes of your soul, and to help spread the Divine Light to humanity and the planet.

Discussion and action create polarities instead of solving them

In your world of divisions, many people strive to create a better world by way of discussion, politics, and action. At first, these seem appropriate ways to create change. However, the path of discussion and action misses an important fact. In your world of divisions, every action creates a counteraction, and every thought creates a thought contrary to itself. Discussion and action are inherently polarized. They do not produce true solutions. Decisions based on harmony and consensus work better than those based on so-called democratic principles.

We do not mean that you should abandon the concept of democracy. Democracy is quite effective at handling—within the rules of the earth plane—the multiple challenges that arise when people with many different visions live together. However, in the long term, a system that transcends polarities would be better. We might call this the *intuitive harmonic way* of making decisions. As you develop your intuitive energy body and live in alignment with your soul, you will develop ways to transcend polarities. This development will occur for individuals as well as for humanity as a whole.

We are talking about a way of developing yourself that works directly with light. The most efficient way to change yourself is to go to the light of your higher self and your multidimensional being. You can also bring in higher energies from the beings of light, the soul of your sun, or the Divine Light. You can do this by meditating and by using the techniques described earlier.

Working with light transcends polarities

The most effective way to change humanity is to work on the level of light *first*—before you participate in discussion and action. However, we do not propose that you only meditate and retreat from the world. The divisions and the polarities of the world also require that you speak words and take action.

Politics would benefit greatly if the whole government would retreat in meditation to receive higher insights on important issues. After that, the politicians could discuss these insights, but not in an argumentative way as they do now. Politics as it is now, with all the different parties, is a clear example of polarity.

Older societies such as Lemuria were governed by a council of light. Some day, your society may again benefit from this divinely inspired system of government. This, however, will only be possible when the consciousness of humanity has reached a higher level. This way of governing works well only if the members of the council are very sensitive to what is going on in society. When this condition is met, government by a council of highly developed spirits is neither autocratic nor dictatorial. In their meditations, the highly developed spirits of the council receive higher guidance and Divine Purpose. They pick up all the people's and society's signals and desires.

If politicians would meditate, world problems could be solved

The Western world is not yet ready to implement a system of government by a council of enlightened ones. A workable system for your present society would be to have all politicians follow a higher path of light. This might teach them to distinguish more clearly between what motivates them on a personality level and what is the higher purpose of the universe.

Few politicians will admit or even recognize that their political motives are mostly personal. Many of your political ideals come from mass thinking. They may also come from the way you were raised. For example, you may have adopted your parent's political ideals when you had a good relationship with them, or rebelled against these ideals when your parents were too strict. You may see that this has little to do with a higher purpose of the universe.

The system of political parties is also a great obstacle to clear vision. You may believe that by adopting the mass thinking of your party, you are striving toward some higher goals. In fact, these ideas are mainly mass personality goals.

We do not say that all politicians are only motivated by their personality goals. Some are not. Some politicians are evolved persons with high ideals. We would prefer that everyone who is involved in politics be on a path of light. That way, all politicians could learn to sense and distinguish between personality goals, and higher goals that reflect the greater plan.

If all those who are involved in government and all politicians would meditate on their personal insights, or on their party's insights, their decisions would be based—to a much greater degree—on higher insights. Debate would entail less argument and more openness to the wisdom that each person would be offering.

Some people seem to be continually involved in discussions about any given topic. Perhaps they sincerely wish to change the world by using mental energy to convince others of something. Often, however, these discussions are just a way for the personality to explore and to experiment with handling the divisional aspects of your world. Since an opinion is always only one side of a division of viewpoints, choosing and defending an opinion may be a way to explore the divisions. Younger souls, especially, greatly enjoy playing with the possibilities inherent in the divisions. Some, who enjoy playing with gravity, choose spectacular sports like surfing or racing. Others enjoy having polarized discussions such as political debates. In a debate, a personality's goal may not be to find the highest solution for all but rather to experience the joy of exploring polarities or the joy of winning.

People who meditate are bringing more and more light down to the earth

With the development of the intuitive energy body, the consciousness of humanity will rise to a level where the principles described here will be understood, shared, and adopted more easily.

When you are working on your own growth, the same principles operate. The highest way to solve an issue is to go inside, find higher guidance, and become more finely attuned to the higher energies. The more finely you are attuned to the higher energies, the more finely you are attuned to the energies of manifesting in your world. If you want to discover what you can do for humanity, or how to help manifest things for humanity, go inside and find higher guidance and light.

When, by going inward and upward, you find light and use it for yourself, you are also giving it to humanity. This process is called bringing down the light. The light of the higher realms has many qualities. Many different frequencies and energies exist, but not all of them are available to humans on the earth plane yet. When you meditate, and explore these frequencies and energies, you make them available to humanity.

When we call these energies light, we are speaking metaphorically. The physical light which you perceive in your world disappears when you switch off the light, whereas the higher light settles down on the earth. People who meditate might be compared to plants that absorb the sunlight and are able to create forms from it.

When you go inward and explore this light in meditation, you also bring it down for humanity. You can make this process even more powerful when you consciously send the light you are receiving out to humanity. In that way, you act like a transformer, finding the light in the higher realms, receiving it, translating it, and then sending it out to humanity. To do this, just have the intention to spread out the light you are receiving. If you feel that some part of humanity, or a certain part of the world, needs a certain quality of light, find this quality of light with your awareness by focusing on it. Next, hold this part of humanity, or this part of the world, in your attention while you open to receive this quality and fill yourself with it. The light you receive in this way will reach the area you choose.

You might send light out to other people or to certain areas. How much of your transmitted light they actually receive depends on how open they are. Transmitting light is best done from a place of neutrality, a place of not pushing to change things. Transmitting light is just offering the light that you feel is needed and letting go of any results. Detaching from the results is difficult for the personality but creates better outcomes than pushing does. The history of humanity, with all its wars and struggles, shows this clearly.

This is the end of this chapter.

***

F: Can I ask a question?

P: Go ahead.

F: If someone sends light to another person, will humanity benefit?

P: If you take a person into your awareness, part of your light is directed toward this person. This has direct or indirect effects on humanity as a whole. All light work you do affects humanity and the planet as a whole. The same principle applies when you work in the earth reality. For example, your giving someone a present affects the planet as a whole, although the effect will be small. If you buy a book, you are using the resources of the earth, for example, the wood that is needed to make the paper for the book. On an energy level, the joy of the person who receives the present affects that person's environment.

EARTH CHANGES

F: I have another question about what you said about the world of divisions when you talked about politics. If we ask the people who play loud music at our campsite to turn the volume down, would that produce a counterreaction?

P: Ideal ways of handling things may differ from more practical ways of handling things. The practical ways may be helpful for less important issues, like your loud music situation. If you only meditate and send light and qualities of harmony to these people, they will take quite a while to pick up your transmissions and change their conceptions about reality and the way they handle things. Your desired results will take much longer to create than the length of time you intend to stay here. Talking to the people might be more practical. However, we suggest that you go inward first and meditate, and see the light in these people and their joy in this music. If you harmonize with their energy in this way, you will find it a lot easier to talk with them about their music in a pleasant manner. As long as you feel angry about their music, they may not listen to your request and they may respond on an energy level with anger. So you see, meditation is still helpful, even in small matters.

P: Does that answer your question?

F: Yes.

P: Do you have any more questions?

F: No.

P: Then we will end our dictation for today and say good-bye to you with all our love and support.

35.
Meditation: Manifesting Light
McBride Springs

Welcome, this is Phylos. We greet you from up high on our mountain and send you a message of love and support through time and space.

1. Find a comfortable position and relax your muscles even more, letting go of tension with each exhalation, drawing light and energy to you with each inhalation. Be aware of your energy, and your thoughts, emotions, and bodily sensations at this moment.

2. As you observe, retreat more and more into that point of observation from where you observe the energy about you. Retreat into the core of your being, into that place of inner silence that is behind your thoughts, emotions, and sensations. From this place of inner silence, observe your energy.

3. See or feel an energetic quality that is common to everything you think, feel, or see. Sense this underlying energy, a base set of frequencies, which is you as you exist in the higher dimensions. Perhaps this underlying energy appears to you as a tone, the base tone that is you.

When you look around a little with your inner eyes, you may notice this base tone in everything you perceive. The frequencies of what you perceive are mingled with the frequencies of your perception. Realize that there is no perception without your perceiving it. What you see in the outer world is your perception and, indeed, your creation.

4. Now concentrate again on the point of inner silence. Just be this inner silence, and from this place, connect with the frequencies of the soul of your sun. Feel its beautiful energy coming into your aura, bringing in life force energy, soothing your aura.

5. Then find the light of the Divine, that wave of light that is basic to All There Is. It is full of purpose. From your point of inner silence, feel the greatness of this light as you receive it. Recognize how this light is present in everything. Notice its presence in all consciousness, in your aura and your body, and in everything in the world. Feel how this strong, loving, beautiful light full of purpose permeates everything.

6. Now open even more to this light. Your space of inner silence is filled with this light now. Feel the peace. Let a wish come into your mind. It may be something you desire for humanity, for another person, or for a group of people, or for a place on the earth. It may also be something you desire for the animal kingdom, or the plants, or the minerals.

7. In this Divine Light, find those frequencies that will help your wish to manifest in the world of matter. You do not have to know how to do this. Just intend to find the right frequencies that make this happen. Keep your attention on this wish and on this set of frequencies at the same time.

This is all you need to do. Do not push anything or try to change anything. Just allow the flow of light, and feel what happens with your energy. Is it getting bigger and more expansive? Are you feeling more joyful perhaps, more tranquil? Observe whatever you can in your energy, perhaps more light or more peace.

8. Now let go of your wish. Let go of those frequencies and

just sit for a while in the light of the Divine and in the light of the soul of your sun. You might feel your aura expanding, as if your intuitive energy body is building.

With this expanded aura, feel the energies about you. Feel that with the intuitive layer in your aura you can feel the energies in your surroundings. Perhaps you experience more ease and more precision in your perception. If plants, animals, or insects are present, feel their energy. See how easily you can pick up these energies with your intuition and how they affect you.

9. Now go back to your ordinary reality, and do so slowly, step by step, in your own way so that all the light you have received is translated to your ordinary reality.

And with that, we say good-bye to you for now with all our love and light.

36.
World Crises

Clear Creek Trail

Welcome, this is Phylos. We send you our love and light from our realms. At this moment, you are walking in the place where we are most at home in your realms. We are grateful that you made the effort to get to this place where you can experience our energies the most intensely.

We were walking on Clear Creek Trail, on the McCloud side of the mountain. The road to the trail had been long and dusty. We had read that Phylos appeared on this side of the mountain in the 1920's.

This is where we walked in human form at the beginning of this century. As we explained earlier, we will not appear in physical form today, but as you tune in to our energies, you may feel that we are closer than ever before.

You are walking in the direction of our Radiant Temple. We will point out its position on the mountain when you are a bit higher on the mountain. There, masters have offered major teachings to humanity.

World crises are a side effect of growing consciousness

As we teach, our lessons change with the period of time and with the development of human consciousness. Our lessons today are mainly about consciousness and how to deal with its expansion, and about the development of the intuitive energy body. In a way, our lessons are less concrete than they were in the past. You have reached a level of growth in which strict guidelines are not so necessary. The consciousness of humanity has evolved to a new level where people have a lot more freedom and many more ways to explore reality. In addition, humanity has developed its ability to handle more freedom and be more respectful of the individual lives of humans, as well as of animals and plants.

You might doubt these words because you see so much chaos and misery in the world about you. Nevertheless, we want to show you the truth of our words. The misery and chaos on the earth are partly the result of the development of consciousness in its state of greater freedom. This development of consciousness continues although human society does not yet have well-developed rules to handle the increased freedom on the earth.

The shift has only started. This is a period of transition during which those people who are not yet open to this light of awakening and expanded consciousness are trying to keep their grip in old ways by using power over others. They do not understand what is happening and cannot deal with this new freedom yet so some misuse it to achieve their own goals.

We have to add here that misusing freedom in this way is not a bad thing. Some people just act this way in the difficult new situation that has emerged on the earth plane. All the chaos and misery in the world, all these crises, are necessary for people to awaken to the new consciousness. Each crisis brings about new thought forms and new consensus about how to handle such earth changes in the future. Increasing numbers of people in this world are awakening. People on all levels are communicating a great deal more with each other.

Chaos and misery disappear when people awaken to their higher vision

When you look about you, you see many beautiful developments. Increasing numbers of people care about each other, about humanity as a whole, and about nature. Their caring is greater than ever. We advise you to put your focus on these positive developments and develop your own consciousness in these ways. Do not let yourself go into fear about imminent catastrophes.

In this new phase of consciousness, you can more easily contact the higher realms and the beings of light, the angels, and masters like us. More and more information from our realms is reaching humanity. We advise you to take note of all this information. Listen to it or read it with your intuition to feel which information is really from the higher realms and which information evolves from the personality of the writer or speaker.

At this time, many wars and other crises exist on the earth. They represent one way of awakening humanity. Another way would be for each of you to learn to use your higher vision to observe your world from a higher perspective. One of the major goals of our teachings is to help each of you and all humanity find this higher vision and develop it further. In the end, the result will be about the same, whether it will have been achieved through crises, or through love and higher vision.

In essence, you are beings of love and your true path is love. All those crises you dislike so much are not humanity's real path. You may find it helpful to know that many big crises are caused by the ignorance of a few souls. Persons who have awakened to a higher level of consciousness do not yet occupy many positions of power. Leaders who have power but who are not yet awake make decisions that mostly serve their personalities. Such decisions may serve their own materialistic goals or protect them against real or imagined threats.

These decisions are profitable only for the short term and may, in the long run, damage humanity and the earth. You can help persons who are in places of power by sending them light and love, and holding a focus for them to awaken to higher levels of consciousness. Eventually, awakened ones will occupy positions of power and leadership.

We hope that you will read these pages with an open heart and with your intuition so that you may experience some of the love we have put into them to help you awaken. We also hope that, while you read our material, you feel the love we transmit to you. Because we come from a realm of no time and space, our love reaches you through time and space. We feel connected to you who are reading this, although from earth perspective, you will read this at another time, in the future.

We say good-bye to you now with deep respect for your being and with our gratitude to you for receiving our teachings.

37.
Visit to Castle Lake: Indian Lives
Little Castle Lake

The day after Phylos gave us the previous chapter, he directed us to a trail past Little Castle Lake, a beautiful, secluded little lake in the Mount Shasta area. He guided us to follow the trail toward a yellowish rock formation.

Welcome, this is Phylos. As you walk now in this beautiful ancient landscape, you may feel the vibrations of older times coming up from this mountain. Humans have dwelled here since ancient times. You now walk on holy grounds of the Native American people. Here, Froukje will have her most profound visions of the past because this was her territory in earlier lives.

We suggest you sit here on these stones. Find a place of power on these rocks. Now close your eyes and connect with the power of the rocks. Feel the energies coming up from them and feel what those energies do to your experience. You may get a sense of well-being. As you sit here on the rocks and feel their energy, let that energy carry you back in time. You may want to go to your place of inner silence first, and from there observe the earlier times. Stop at points of particular interest. When you are ready, you can start speaking. Froukje, just describe what you perceive.

***

F: I see a Native American woman.

P: We suggest you start by describing her clothes and appearance.

F: She has dark hair, brown eyes. She is small but strong. She is wearing some kind of dress.

P: Do you know her?

F: I think this woman is me.

P: Do you know her name?

F: Something like Gwendala.

P: How is Gwendala feeling?

F: She is feeling fine.

P: What is she doing?

F: She is looking out over the valley. She feels strong, well in her body, and healthy. She is very flexible in her movements.

"We suggest you sit here on these stones."

P: What does she do in this lifetime?

F: She enjoys being in nature, connecting with the earth and with outdoor life. She feels very happy in her community.

P: Good. Do you want to explore this life further? Perhaps go to this community and describe it?

F: I see a circle of tents. Everybody lives in a circle around a central place. There are children.

P: Anything else?

F: An old woman lives where Gwendala lives. She is a wise, old woman.

P: All right, you are doing fine. You might go into that if you wish.

F: A strong connection exists between this older woman and me.

P: If you want to learn more about this life, you might concentrate on the details of what you see. They serve as vehicles that help you go further into this life.

F: I see the face of the older woman and her thin, gray hair. Her face has many wrinkles. She has wise, calm-looking eyes in an oval face that is quite big. Her hair is in a ponytail. She has earrings with holes in them.

P: Maybe she will talk to you. Listen to what she says, and tell us.

F: She puts her hand on my heart and says, "I give you my wisdom."

P: What is her name? What else does she say or do?

F: She loves me a lot. She says she is going to die soon, and she wants to give me her wisdom and her knowledge about healing and about plants for healing.

P: Maybe you can go deeper into your impressions. Maybe she has something to teach you.

F: I see her treating someone, singing songs, asking the spirits for help, dancing and singing. She makes special movements and rhythms.

Now she works with her hands on the body of the person

she is treating. She moves the legs and the body in a kind of pulsing movement, working with special points on the body.

P: Do you see any of these points? Where are they located?

F: In the neck and further down on the back. She is working in lines down the back, going to the buttocks, and then to the legs.

P: Good. Since she gave you her wisdom, you might go further into this, maybe to a later age of her life. So concentrate again on your point of silence. Feel the power of these rocks and the energy of this place. Go forward a little in time, until you yourself are a wise woman. When you are there, connect with what is happening at that moment. Describe what you feel or see. What you see is important. Just describe whatever comes into your mind.

F: Now I have my hair in two ponytails, and I am working with medicinal plants. I think I also see auras around plants.

P: What do they look like?

F: Like etheric bodies of different colors around each plant. The colors tell me if the plants are good for healing.

P: Which colors are good? What do you see that makes the difference?

F: When the colors are too intense, like a bright red, they are too dangerous to use. But when they are light blue or light yellow, I can use them for healing.

P: You are still doing great.

F: Now I see myself healing someone. I can also see the aura of the person I am healing.

P: Tell more about it.

F: I can see that this person has a problem in the lower back. The red colors there are too strong. So I work with my hands to get these colors to the outside of the aura, and bring in more light, more soft colors, blue and yellow and soft blue.

EARTH CHANGES

P: Well now, concentrate on the healing power you have in this lifetime as a Native American woman. Let this feeling, this knowing, permeate all of your body, aura, and cells. Let your body's memory and your aura's memory grow as strong as possible while you release the images of this time. Then connect with this rock again, feeling its healing power.

Now, go forward in time until you are back in the here and now. Feel how some of the ability to heal has come back with you through time, as a resource from the past. You may use this ability to heal more easily now, as you are more able to see or sense the colors in the auras of your clients and work with them. Maybe other intuitive knowledge has come back also.

The gifts of intuition and of seeing auras began to be developed in ancient times. In those times, these gifts were given to only a few and took a lot of effort to develop. These powers will be revealed to more and more people during humanity's next phase of growth. As the intuitive energy body develops, your inner senses will develop and you will develop more of these powers. At first, you may notice that you see colors more deeply. Even as this begins, you may experience a vague sense or intuitive knowing about what is happening with other people. These days, you can already develop your clairvoyance a great deal more than many believe.

F: How can I do that now?

P: One way is to bring your awareness back to this rock and to this lifetime in which you already possessed these skills. Then bring them back to your current lifetime. Bring back even more than you just did. You can further develop these talents by meditating and sensing. Do you have any more questions?

F: No.

P: Then for now we thank you for helping us illustrate our point. We say good-bye to you for now with all our love and light.

38.
Meditation: Absorbing Light

Saint Germain's Spring, Upper Panther Meadow

We were sitting at the spring of the small mountain stream at Upper Panther Meadow. This spring is sacred to Native Americans. Saint Germain appeared here in 1930 to the writer, Guy Ballard.[9]

Welcome. This is Phylos greeting you from this place of high energy and holiness. This meditation is about absorbing light.

1. Imagine that you are in a most beautiful meadow, radiant with energy, a true meadow of the masters. As you sit relaxed, with closed eyes, imagine this beautiful place, with rocks, flowers, and water. Lovely, ice-cold, mountain water bubbles up out of a spring and flows all over the meadow. Feel the holiness of this place. You might see or imagine a soft golden light. Everything is shining, every organism and every rock of this meadow, shining with a soft, golden, radiant light.

2. Now imagine that the spring is an energy entrance into the earth. Let yourself be drawn into the spring and then through it into the earth, as if you were very small. Instead of darkness, a vast space is opening for you, a place of light. Bring all of your attention into this vast space of light. Feel yourself floating in this light, and feel the holiness of the energies here.

3. Then, within this light notice certain clusters of energy. You might see them floating by. The longer you are here, the more concrete the images become, as if they are islands of light floating through this vastness. Let yourself float toward such an island of light until you are on this island. Look around at the world you are now in. It may or may not look familiar to you. It is more ethereal than your world, and forms are less defined. You can see forms, but their boundaries are not so discernable. This is more like a world of light.

4. Let the images in this world become clearer. You may perceive soft colors, forms, and moving images of beings.

Let one of these beings approach you now. As it approaches, its form starts to become clearer. Look at this being's light and fluidity. Feel how you can communicate with this being in this vast world of light. Maybe the being has a message for you, or a gift of light. Accept this message or gift now. Take all the time you want to connect with this being. Then, say good-bye and let go of the energy of this island of light.

5. Let yourself float in this vastness again until you find a stream of colored energies. When you find this stream, let yourself be carried by the stream. You move faster and faster with this stream. The stream takes you to a place where the masters meet. Imagine that you are arriving at this place right now.

6. Look around at this beautiful place. Maybe you see familiar shapes like rocks and mountains, but again they are much more light-filled than usual, their beautiful, shining colors ever changing. Just sit here for a while and absorb this light. Feel all these colors of light in your aura and in your body.

7. Open even more to receive this very special light from galaxies far away, a light that has not yet been established on

the earth plane. The more people who do this meditation, the more of this light will be brought to the earth plane.

8. Feel the special quality of this light, its softness, and its high energy. You may feel as though you could live just on this light alone because it gives you everything you need on the physical level and also on the soul level. It is a nourishing light. Let your cells open to this light. Your cells are drinking in this light and are shining with this light. You might feel that you are evolving into new levels of physical fitness and health.

9. Concentrate on the quality of feeling healthy, whatever that means to you at this moment. Concentrate, and imagine how the energy of a completely healthy body feels. Feel how the light of this place intermingles with this energy of health and energizes it. A new light blends with the light of health, and the energy of health is becoming more tangible. Every cell and structure of your body absorbs this light and so does your aura. Vibrant health and high energy radiate from your body. Feel the potential in this energy, like that of a spring flowing out of a mountain, a new energy, bringing new life, new ideas, and new visions. Feel it opening new possibilities in your life.

10. Feel how your mental energy body becomes clearer, and how your thoughts light up with this light as they become more complete and more precise. Also feel this light in your memory bank, so to speak. Feel how this light makes it easier to access your memories, as thought it were bringing new order into your stored memories.

11. Concentrate on how this light works in your emotional energy body. Notice how your emotions become clearer. Your intuitive energy body also opens and receives this light and shines more and more. See how all these structures interact: the memory, the mental energy body, the emotional energy body, the physical body, and the intuitive energy body. See

how rays of light move quickly between these layers, more and more quickly. Many rays of light emerge, disappear, and come back again, so that the interaction between your energy bodies becomes clearer and more orderly. Each energy body is independent of the others and at the same time, they all interact with each other more and more. They are separate and yet one.

12. Now, vibrating with the new light of the masters, you may return by imagining you are coming out of the spring, back into the meadow. As you do so, take all of this light and all of your experiences with you, easily integrating them here on this meadow. When you come back and open your eyes, be aware of how vibrant you are, and how you radiate this new energy. Be aware of your growing health and your ability to be nourished by the Divine Light.

We say good-bye to you now with all our love and light.

39.
Earth Changes
Dead Fall Meadows

Welcome, this is Phylos, greeting you with love and support. This chapter is about earth changes.

As we have mentioned before, the energies in the world are presently undergoing some major changes and developments. In order to prepare you for these shifts in energy and for the development of your intuitive energy body, we have taught you some methods of going inside to develop your inner senses and expand your consciousness.

Meditation develops your inner senses and starts the process of dissolving the illusions that your normal senses give you about your world. Meditation and the exercises we have given you can take you to the planes of higher light and help you bring this light back to the earth where you can transmit it to humanity.

New visions are emerging because of changes in the energies on the earth

The earth changes we are talking about have already started. In fact, they started in the late Sixties. The new energies that have been coming to the earth have caused these changes. These energies will be felt most strongly around 2012.

This stream of energy will result in a major change in consciousness for humanity and for the plant and animal kingdoms. The whole earth plane will vibrate with a new energy and will be filled with a new potential. Increasing numbers of people are starting to meditate or otherwise work on their spiritual growth. Cynics may say that people need a new sense of security because the great Western religions are declining. However, the real reason for the decline of the major religions and the emergence of new visions is the change in the energy on the earth.

The teachings of the main religions have been very beneficial to the world. People who live in accordance with these teaching as they were originally intended provide enormous support for humanity's shift in consciousness. Unfortunately, as the energies changed more and more during the last centuries, the religions became more fear-based and thus more rigid. Often the old religions are no longer in harmony with the new energies, which demand greater flexibility.

Compare the basic teachings of the older religions with the concepts underlying the new spiritual visions of today and you will see that they do not disagree at all. Disagreement only exists at the mental level. When you read the texts and teachings with your intuition and your emotional energy body, you will find that the basic principals have been the same throughout time. Differences arise only when humans begin discussing the teachings, interpreting them with the mental energy body. This use of the mental energy body originates in survival mechanisms. The fear involved in the survival mechanisms creates even sharper differences between the teachings of the various religions, and even leads to wars.

Cynics say that people turn toward new visions, meditation, and adopt religious beliefs because their personalities need

EARTH CHANGES

affection or explanations for unanswerable questions. But, in truth, people are changing because the energies on the earth are changing to a higher frequency. When you follow the flow of the new energies, you will discover an inner drive to learn about these new energies. Because the earth energies are more fluid now, many more different spiritual pathways exist now than existed in the past.

The energy shift that is changing your earth now is not the first great energy shift that has come to the earth plane. Many shifts have preceded this one. We are not talking here about small energy changes that occur moment to moment, but about big energy shifts that deeply affect the consciousness of the whole planet.

Major shifts in energy give birth to new religions which can meet the needs of the new energies. This has happened many times in the past and is now happening again. At this moment, however, as the energies become increasingly fluid and of a higher frequency, not just one central religion is arising. On the contrary, many new groups, small and large, are emerging, each emphasizing different aspects of the awakening consciousness brought about by these energies. Some people are experiencing this as a chaotic period while others are exited by all the new possibilities and choices.

You have knowledge of the last few thousand years of your history, but highly developed civilizations already existed hundreds of thousands of years ago. You will find very few remains of those civilizations, except for a few phenomena that may puzzle you, such as the stones on Easter Island. Major energy shifts also occurred during the times of these early civilizations. Consider the metaphor of the spiraling form of time. When a civilization has risen and declined, another spiral in time is completed. At this moment, another spiral has almost been completed and the next one is starting at a higher level.

Divine masters are incarnating to help humanity with the shift in consciousness

When great energy shifts occur, divine persons incarnate to help humanity with the resulting change in consciousness. Divine incarnations, or avatars, come to the earth for two purposes. First, they have a great capacity to connect with the light of the new energy waves and bring it down to earth. In this way, diffuse light becomes more condensed so that the earth and its inhabitants will be able to use it. Secondly, avatars can make these energies available to humans and help people to adapt to these energies.

If you have an opportunity, we recommend that you connect with such avatars. Although we could give you names of avatars, we suggest that you use your developing intuitive energy body to sense who are the real avatars.

A few guidelines may help you. Real avatars never impose rules on their followers. Moreover, you are free to come and go with them; they do not pressure you to follow their doctrine. Their doctrine itself is not rigid. It respects the individual at a deep level.

We give you these guidelines because some people think they are avatars but they are not. We do not mean you cannot learn anything from these persons. It is important to use your intuition in all of your decisions and especially in decisions about your path of spiritual growth.

Your developing intuitive energy body may cause growing pains

EARTH CHANGES

As you adapt to the new energy coming to earth, it is also important for you to follow your own flow at all levels. You will find this to be even more important later than it is now. As this energy becomes stronger, you will clearly feel what is right for you and what is not. In the beginning, you may experience growing pains in your increasing intuition. You will probably become far more sensitive to energies and atmospheres.

Some of you are already very sensitive now. Sometimes you may feel less grown up than before, as if you have more difficulty being around people you do not like or being in energies you do not like. Once these people and energies presented no problems for you. But now when you are in such atmospheres or energies, you may even react with physical or emotional complaints. If you are on your path of inner growth, sometimes things may seem to be getting worse instead of better. For example, you might be more emotional and feel more vulnerable. Emotions may come more quickly and you may not quite understand why. On the physical level, old pains may reemerge or you may develop new pains.

We hope you will not be discouraged by these symptoms but instead learn to welcome them as signs of your developing intuition. As your intuitive energy body gets stronger, these growing pains will diminish. They are signs of your rapid growth process. Do not go to your doctor or psychiatrist too quickly, but try to be open to these feelings. Just observe them and let them be. That way you will quickly discover whether your complaints are caused by your intuition and feelings, or whether they are caused by other factors. The latter may be the case when you cannot discover a pattern underlying your complaints.

Some symptoms are the result of both your feelings and your intuition in addition to other factors. This might be the situation when parts of your physical body, which gave you a problem in the past and afterward felt fine, now suddenly feel painful again.

It is increasingly important to find your higher flow

With the development of the intuitive energy body and arrival of the new energies on the earth, you need to follow your intuition more precisely to determine what you do or do not want to do and where you do or do not want to be. People, places, and activities of higher energy will be good for you while those of lower energies will give you a great deal of difficulty. This will become increasingly important as the energy waves become stronger.

Therefore, people will virtually be forced to choose a higher path. To say they are being forced is perhaps not quite accurate: after all, when they choose their higher path, they are choosing their soul's path, which is the path that gives them the most joy, freedom, and abundance.

At this time, quite a few of you are experiencing yourselves in a void. You may still have difficulty knowing and deciding what to do. Or you may feel that you lack the resources to do what you want to do.

In these teachings, we cannot explore what causes each individual to experience the void. You may experience the void because you are too mental, even though you are on a path of growth. You may feel very enthusiastic about all kinds of things you read or hear, but the most important thing for you to do may be to allow your intuitive energy body to develop more.

We will not give detailed guidance here, but you might consider doing spontaneous things—like just going somewhere and following your intuition about what to do there. If you are a person who is trying to control life by doing a lot of planning because you feel that this is the best way to keep a grip on things, try to let go of this pattern and become more flowing. You might take a holiday, for example, and without planning anything follow your intuition regarding where you want to go and what you want to do.

No matter what your level of development, you will always have lessons on the earth plane level.

As you develop your intuitive energy body, you may have difficulty staying grounded. That is, you might have difficulty staying connected to the energies of the earth. On a practical level, being grounded means having a job and doing all kinds of earthly things.

If you are already quite developed spiritually, you might not enjoy earthly activities anymore because you feel they are of a lower energy. In that case, your spiritual growth may be a bit too fast for your soul's purposes on the earth plane. Perhaps your soul's lessons on the earth plane level were not always joyful so you wished to avoid them. For example, your soul may have chosen an experience from which you could learn a lot like an illness or an accident. However, the personality would see these situations as undesirable, requiring an immediate remedy or resolution.

If you concentrate only on developing higher spiritual qualities, you may overlook the fact that your soul may want you to learn certain lessons about life on earth. This is especially the case when your spiritual growth is ahead of your earth growth. By earth growth, we mean the lessons that ground you more and bring you into greater contact with the earth.

When you follow your higher path, your lessons are generally not as harsh anymore. This does not mean you should retreat from earthly things. Your soul created a life on the earth plane, and the purpose of that life is to work with the energies and circumstances of earth.

Sometimes you may discover that things you did not enjoy or circumstances you did not want to be in, taught you valuable qualities that are important for your higher path. You may have a job that does not seem to fit you, but that helps you develop certain qualities, such as patience or endurance.

Perhaps you have been involved in activities that do not seem to be high at all and that you may later dislike, such as drinking too much alcohol in a pub. Such activities may help you to discover what life on the earth plane is all about and to develop your strength. No matter what you are doing and why you are doing it, the important thing is to learn to be conscious while doing it. Possibly going to a pub and maybe even getting drunk was a good way for you to learn how to become more grounded.

When you are clear about what your soul is telling you, its choices and interventions will become less drastic and more supportive to your being. You may then see, for example, that you do not need to get drunk at all, and that you feel much stronger by resisting alcohol in the pub.

Perhaps, in retrospect, you dislike an activity or experience in your past. Or you dislike an activity or experience in your present. Try to find the higher purpose of the activity or experience. Think about what you may have been learning from your soul's perspective. If the lesson is about developing a specific quality, you might find other ways to develop that quality, ways that are more supportive to your being.

Sometimes it may be good for you to do activities that

EARTH CHANGES

do not seem to fit your higher path at all. They may serve a purpose for your soul development. You might think that hiking or participating in sports is a higher way of becoming grounded than visiting a pub. Of course, hiking or sports can connect you to the earth very well, but perhaps you are already a good athlete and have been hiking since you were a child. In that case, hiking or sports may hold no challenge for you. Often your soul wants you to develop additional qualities and new ways to increase your connection with the earth.

We cannot go into all the individual causes and problems of unbalanced growth, but we hope this gives you something to consider when you look at your own life.

The new energies coming to the earth will make it easier for the soul to learn on the earth plane because the connection between the personality and the soul will be more open. People will care more for each other and for the earth, creating greater beauty and harmony. The earth will be a much safer place to be because there will be no more war. Increased harmony among humans, and between humans and the earth, will result in fewer crises and natural disasters.

We cannot say, however, that it will be without struggle, the paradise that some people fantasize. After all, you are on the earth plane to learn certain things. This requires an environment in which you can learn. Without tension or challenge, you cannot learn much. However, it will be a much better world.

This is the end of this chapter. We say good-bye to you now with our deepest love and light.

40.
At Last, We Visit Medicine Lake
Little Medicine Lake

During this visit to Mount Shasta, we finally made it to Medicine Lake. We felt the flow was leading us there. When we arrived after a long drive, we did not like the area at all. We took a walk, but we both felt tired and did not like the flat and dusty landscape. We found it quite boring. We could not walk around the lake anymore since one side of it had been developed and was now owned by a few people. We sat down beside a small nearby lake called Little Medicine Lake.

Welcome, this is Phylos. We greet you with a message of love and support. You are puzzled about why we brought you here because you feel that the energy here is low indeed. The energies here are contradictory. When you bathe in Medicine Lake, you may receive a special energy gift. The great lake still contains some of the old power; swimming in it is good for fertility. What you feel here is the accumulated karma of this area. As you close your eyes and go back in time to when the Native Americans still inhabited it, you may experience the energy of this place differently. In fact, this was once a place of high energy. After white people occupied it and destroyed its glow of beauty, the energy was drawn back into the earth.

Our first reason for taking you here is to develop your

intuition. The book you bought about sacred sites describes this as a place of high energy, and you both correctly feel that this is a place of low energy. Your sensing of energy is developing. It is good to feel this contrast. Our other reason for taking you here is to make it possible for you to take a swim in the lake and receive some of the old powers that are contained in it. You will probably feel this when you are in the water. The lake gives your physical body healing. In addition, after you connect with the energy of the lake and absorb it into your system, you may take it with you to use it for yourself and others.

Right now, close your eyes and go back in time, picking up the energy of this place a few hundred years ago. Maybe you can describe what images come up.

***

F: I see Native Americans swimming in the lake and having fun with children. I see a man with a feather headdress, long black hair, and a bit of a hawk-nose looking out over the lake.

P: What is he doing there?

F: I think he is looking for animals to hunt.

P: How is the energy of the place?

F: The energy feels light and bright.

P: At this moment, it is not that important to go into these pictures more deeply because what we want both of you to do is to feel the energy of that time and compare it with the energy of this time. You may feel that the energy was much higher and lighter at that time.

The main purpose of your visit is to swim in the lake. When you do, do so consciously. We suggest that you go underwater completely three times to connect with the powers of the lake and to bring them into your systems so that you bring them with you when you come out again.

EARTH CHANGES

For now, we say good-bye to you with all our love and gratitude for all the work you are doing.

We did as Phylos said, had a swim and submerged ourselves three times. We enjoyed the swim and felt refreshed. As soon as we were dry again, we drove back to the campground at Mount Shasta as we still did not like the Medicine Lake area very much. In the evening, Phylos commented about our experience and led us in a meditation about it.

Welcome again. You did well this afternoon when you went into Medicine Lake and concentrated on the power of the water. At a conscious level, you may not have experienced all the power, but at a subconscious level you did. Your long journey today was an important one indeed.

We asked that you submerge yourselves in the water of the water three times. This is the first time we have introduced some kind of a ritual. Maybe we will do a chapter on ancient knowledge and rituals one of these days.

Now we will guide you into a meditation.

41.
Revitalizing Meditation
McBride Springs

Welcome, this is Phylos.

1. Imagine that you are standing in a very special lake, a lake that has been used for ages both for pleasure and for healing, a lake with special powers for those who know about its powers. Beautiful, high-energy, volcanic mountains surround the lake. As you stand there, feel the temperature of the water. Maybe it seems a bit cold at first, but once you are completely submerged in it, it is very refreshing and gives your body vibrant energy.

Feel the difference between this water and the water of a normal lake. Feel the energy of this special water.

2. Let yourself go into the water. Feel the first little shiver when you go in, notice your breath, and feel the chill of your body. Feel the excitement the water gives you, and how this special water carries your whole body. You may swim a bit so that you feel comfortable.

Then, at a place where you can still stand, submerge your whole body including your head. Imagine now that you are completely under water, with your eyes open. Imagine that you can breathe and see normally in this water.

See the green and yellow glow of the light through the

water. Feel how this healing water is all around you, touching your skin, touching every part of your body.

3. Feel the energy of the water coming into your body through your skin. Enjoy this refreshing, revitalizing energy as you absorb it with your whole body. You may also feel the ancient powers of the depths of the lake. After a while, come up again and look around over this beautiful lake. See the shores, and feel the air on your skin as you stand up again.

4. Now go into the water and again submerge your whole body and head. Feel the healing energy and absorb the power of the water through your skin. When you are totally submerged, you may find it amazing how much power and energy the water can transmit to you. Feel this energy and absorb it even more than you did the first time, maybe at a deeper level, refreshing, rejuvenating, and revitalizing you. See the beautiful rays of the sun shining through the water. Feel the energy of the sun as it is transmitted to you through the water. After a while, come up again, and feel the wind and the sun on your skin. Inhale, and enjoy the fresh air.

5. Now, submerge your whole body and head for a third time. Relax completely in the power of the water. You may even feel how the earth underneath feeds this water with energy. This power was brought here by ancient, extinct civilizations that left their energy marks here—to be discovered only by those who know about such energies and are open to experiencing them.

6. Come up again, and slowly go to the shore. Feel the wind and the sun on your whole body. You feel refreshed and relaxed. Inhale the fresh mountain air, and feel your body tingle. Feel a sparkling all over the outside of your body and inside your body, a sparkling of energy throughout. At a deeper level, you may feel how you received transmissions of energy as well as of the ancient knowledge and healing powers that are

contained in this water. These powers will find a place in your system so that you may use them for yourself and others.

7. Slowly, at your own pace, come back to your own time and space, feeling energetic, revitalized, and full of energy and health. We say good-bye to you for now with all our love and light.

42.
Remembering Your Higher State Throughout the Day

Gray Butte Trail

Welcome, this is Phylos. With every step you climb, we are able to transmit more of our energies and information. This chapter is about remembering your higher state throughout the day.

In order to be able to live in a physical body on the earth plane, you use your physical senses and survival mechanisms. With your senses, you see, feel, hear, smell, and taste within the range of frequencies which your senses are equipped to receive. Also, your thoughts come and go in a way of thinking that uses divisions.

Connect with your higher self often during the day

When you start meditating and doing our exercises, and maybe other exercises like these, you expand the range of what your senses can perceive and the way you think. One of the highest ways of thinking is to be thoughtless. In that state, higher frequencies and higher thoughts can come into your mental energy body as energy and translate into more discernable thoughts later.

As you meditate, exercise, or otherwise work on your

spiritual growth, you direct your attention inward and upward to the light and to the energies of the universe, and not to the outer world as you usually do. This produces growth, which fortunately is not lost when you finish the exercise or meditation, so you do not have to start from the beginning each time.

You feel this growth with your inner senses. You may notice that you feel more balanced, harmonized, loving, and at peace. These are signs that you are on your higher path and that you are increasingly listening to the whispers of your soul. You might also feel that you enjoy things like nature, quietness, music, or art at a deeper level.

The more you are able to remember your higher state throughout the day, the more rapidly you will grow, and the more you will live your higher state throughout the day. When you remember your higher state throughout the day, your daily activities increasingly become meditations guided by your soul.

The challenge is to accomplish this. We have some recommendations that may help you live your day in greater accord with your soul. However, these recommendations are not in alignment with how most of your society operates and may be difficult to follow if you have a regular job.

Your mental energy body needs to rest every twenty to thirty minutes

First, we suggest that you not use your mental energy body for periods longer than twenty to thirty minutes. If you are working on your growth, you may feel that activities like reading newspapers or magazines, watching television, or working with a computer make you tired more quickly than they used to. All these activities involve the mental body to a great degree. When you work longer than this, of course, the mental energy body will continue to function. However, during the first twenty minutes, the mental energy body and also the emotional and intuitive energy bodies are involved. A certain balance exists between your energy bodies. With longer periods of mental activity, your mental energy body becomes too prominent and the balance is lost.

If you work for longer periods, your creativity and your problem-solving capacity may decline. Later, while you are doing something completely different like taking a walk or going to sleep, you may suddenly get new ideas or find solutions to problems again. Non-mental activity allows the mental body to relax This opens it to that fifteen percent of your thoughts that you normally neglect—higher creativity, higher inspirations: the whispers of your soul.

You can also overburden your mental body by playing computer and other games that demand a great deal of prolonged concentration. When you stop, you may feel estranged from the world because your mental energy body is overloaded.

For these reasons, we recommend that you do not do mental activities for longer than twenty to thirty minutes at a time and then do some non-mental activities for at least an equal amount of time. You can measure how well you are doing by how tired you feel after a day's work, or how joyful you feel during and after your activities.

More frequent and shorter episodes of sleep balance your waking and sleeping consciousness

Second, we come to the topic of sleep. During sleep, you

access states of consciousness that you cannot access while you are awake. In ancient times, people did not sleep all night and stay awake all day. Because of the possible dangers, people were more alert, as animals are. They slept in shorter episodes, with a more rapid cycling of states of sleep. You can learn a lot about sleeping and being awake by looking at your cat or dog. Your body is constructed in such a way that you feel best when you sleep for a while during the day and for a while during the night, but not necessarily the whole night through. In fact, you feel more rested if you sleep less at night and have one or two short naps during the day.

This may seem more like advice to keep you healthy than advice to develop your consciousness and spiritual growth. However, when you live healthily and, most importantly, in alignment with your soul's needs, you will find it much easier to live according to the higher purposes of your soul. If you follow these two recommendations, your life will improve and you will be more receptive to the messages of your soul.

Do everything you do with full attention

Third, we suggest you do one thing at a time—as calmly as you can. Cooking is a good example of this. If you want to create a really nice meal, begin by cleaning the whole kitchen sink area and freeing it of dishes and clutter. Then put out everything you need for the meal. Prepare each ingredient individually, one after another, vegetable after vegetable. Start cooking only after you have completed all the preparations. Cooking in this way helps you expand your consciousness. Of course, you can also expand your consciousness in many other ways. For instance, when you are at work, do only one thing at a time—calmly.

Connect with the higher energies at least ten times during the day

Now we will talk about how to remember your higher state throughout the day. If you have time, you may start the day with a meditation. When you take a break, you may visualize a golden glow around you. You might also do this when you are meditating. When you do this in meditation and in moments of rest, you remember and get back to your meditative state quickly and easily.

Also, observe nature, listen to nice music, or look at works of art. Take time to find the beauty in your environment. Even better, at all times see the beauty in each person who is with you. Great growth occurs when you concentrate on the beauty of every person you meet or think about. In this way, you also send light and support to these persons. If they receive it, your own light will grow even more.

Is it not wonderful that some of the best ways to grow involve having good thoughts and enjoying people, animals, plants, nature and other things? These practices will have spin-offs in your daily life. You will find yourself more focused, more balanced, and more self-confident. The work you do will improve a lot.

You can also do other things to remember your higher state throughout the day: Write down positive statements or positive thoughts at certain times during the day. You might also write down positive statements about yourself and consciously reflect on them. Examples are: I am a being of light, My soul is guiding me, and so on.

We have mentioned some ways you can remember your higher state throughout the day; many others exist. Some will be easier to implement in your life than others. Use your creativity to discover your own. The main point we want to make is that if you work on your growth in simple, practical ways throughout the day, your growth will be accelerated and more beautiful.

***

F: I have a question. How many hours should we sleep during the night and during the day?

P: We deliberately did not give a number of hours as we do not want to create rigidity. The amount of sleep you need depends on your pattern of sleep, your activities, and the energies that are present. Again, look at your dog or cat and see how it has a rhythm as well as a lot of flexibility in its sleep patterns.

Generally speaking, however, you need less sleep when you change your patterns and become more aligned with your body's rhythms. At first when you change your sleep patterns, you may have difficulty getting a sense of how much sleep you need and when you need it. This is one of the many ways in which you have lost part of your natural feeling of connection with what you really need. When you are able to sleep and be awake in a pattern that is in subtle attunement with the needs of your physical body, you will feel clearer about when you need to sleep and when you want to stay awake. We do know, however, that for most of you the practical ways in which you arrange your lives make this a challenging recommendation.

F: How can I best change my sleep rhythm?

P: First, you will have to get rid of your mental ideas about sleep and about feeling rested or tired. Feeling rested or tired has more to do with the rigidity or fluidity of the mental energy body than with the amount of sleep you actually need. Try to let go of your ideas about how much sleep you need.

Experience may have shown you that sleeping too long can leave you more tired than sleeping too little.

How deeply you sleep varies a lot from night to night. When you sleep for a longer period, the period of deep sleep is about the same as when you sleep for a shorter period.

When you sleep longer, you are not necessarily resting more. Therefore, the first step is to change your ideas about sleep.

Second, when most people wake up at night they immediately try to get to sleep again. However, often if you just stay awake, you will find that the time you spend awake is a time of high energy during which your intuitive energy body is open and ideas may come in. When you wake up, do not try to fall asleep again, but enjoy being awake.

Third, you might want to wake up earlier or go to bed later. Mass thinking suggests that your physical body works better when you live as regularly as possible, eat at fixed times, and sleep at fixed times. In a way, this is true because this conditions you to regularity. However, your life will become a bit dull if you never change anything.

You may have noticed how time seems to pass by quickly in your routine working life, but while you are on holidays, you feel alive and time has a different quality. Changing the times you go to sleep and wake up keeps your body healthier than living according to routine. If you are used to a regular way of living, change may not be easy to accomplish. My suggestion is to experiment with this without changing your whole life at once. You might change one habit a day, without making this change into a new habit. Did this answer your questions?

F: Yes

P: Then I say good-bye to you for now with all my love and support.

43.
Rituals and Ancient Knowledge
Ski Bowl Trail

Welcome, this is Phylos. We connect with you once again from our realms. The book is almost finished. We only have this chapter about rituals and ancient knowledge left to give you.

During the Medicine Lake meditation and while you were actually swimming in Medicine Lake, we asked you to submerge yourself in the water three times. This ritual was useful in finding your higher path. Rituals can have a strong function in guiding your attention towards the higher forces of the universe.

A ritual distracts your attention from the mental and connects you with the higher forces

The more complex a ritual is, the more it distracts your mind from your daily life. There are two kinds of rituals. The first is the *complex ritual* that has the function we just mentioned. The other is what we will call the *sustained ritual*, which is not complicated: it is the continuous repetition of the same thing. Examples are trance drumming or mantra singing. The mind is kept on one track and can easily disregard distractions, focusing awareness back on the sustained ritual.

This brings the mind into a trance state, which is somewhat similar to the state of meditation but may be even deeper.

We do not teach rituals, except for a few simple ones. Rituals have the same pitfall as do religious texts and other ancient knowledge: when they are passed on and on, their essence is difficult to preserve. Often the original function of the ritual, to get in touch with the higher forces and reach states of trance and bliss, is forgotten. The ritual becomes more of a mental process, while its original context no longer exists. People who perform these rituals from a mental base may have good intentions, but to them the rules of the ritual may be more important than its purpose.

These days, with waves of new energy coming to the earth plane, people who are awakening their intuitive energy bodies may feel attracted to rituals. Sometimes new rituals are developed, and sometimes people try to rediscover the ancient knowledge. We recommend that if you want to rediscover rituals, maybe in books or elsewhere, you try to feel the value of the ritual with your intuition. Even when a ritual is described in ancient books, a particular form may no longer be valid for today's energies. In that case, you would do better to adapt it to find its original essence. However, there are also timeless rituals, the power of which you will only feel if you leave them as they are.

Use your intuitive energy body and not your mental energy body to find out how to work with rituals. To find out if you are doing a ritual correctly, look at what it gives you. Does it give you a sense of growth, a feeling of well-being?

The first phase of every ritual you perform will inevitably involve your mental body. You can only measure the ritual's results after this phase. Complex rituals require that you rehearse the patterns mentally until they are yours. With sustained rituals, you have to build the techniques and develop the power so you build up the endurance to perform the ritual for an extended period of time. At first, when you practice an endurance sport as a sustained ritual, your mental body and sometimes also your emotional and physical bodies will find it difficult. To really receive value from the ritual, you just have to go through this phase.

In the times to come, much of the ancient knowledge will be rediscovered

Now we will speak about ancient knowledge. A lot of knowledge about the powers of nature and about different dimensions exists on your earth plane. Some of this knowledge was only valuable at the time it was discovered, and some of this knowledge is still valuable today. Much of this knowledge has been passed on orally in tribal situations, sometimes in very secret ways to keep it pure and protect it from people who may misuse it, perhaps for political purposes.

Unfortunately, this intuitive knowledge was often wiped out with the rapid development of the mental energy body, but much of it is still available. People just stopped paying attention to intuitive knowledge, did not teach it in school, and even denigrated such knowledge. They referred to those who were still in touch with intuitive knowledge as "primitive" or gave them other negative labels. Many other tragedies occurred. People who possessed the old knowledge were often killed or declared mad. Much of the old information may be rediscovered in the coming times.

You cannot imagine how many mysteries on the earth are still waiting to be discovered. A mystery, by its very essence, cannot be easily understood. If you are committed to your growth, however, you may experience some of the miracles that some of these mysteries can evoke when they are unveiled.

The greatest scientific discoveries are still to come

Since many more energies and frequencies than you can perceive with your senses exist on the earth plane, many more possible realities than you can perceive also exist. At this very moment, you share the place where you are with many beings and energies from the past, present, and future —without ever noticing their presence. Constantly, numerous energies—like radio waves, for example—move unnoticed through your auras and physical body. So do many other kinds of energies, most of which your scientists have not yet discovered. They may discover some of these energies in the future. Many of these energies exist in different dimensions. People will only be able to experience these energies when the human intuitive body is more developed.

Bring mystery and magic back into your life

How do you develop your intuitive energy body? One important step is to make your world magical again. Your parents and educational system have taught you to be rational and skeptical. Even persons who are dedicated to their growth will occasionally experience skepticism. Being skeptical and rational will not bring you true happiness and fulfillment. True happiness and fulfillment come when you make your world magical again. You will have to change your beliefs about what in this world is real and what is not. You can, in part, take this step consciously. You can just decide that from now on you will be open to the magical aspects of the world.

EARTH CHANGES

Many people, including those who are religious, already do this. However, people can no longer cling to the old religions for they are not aligned with today's energies. Mental ways of looking at religion, with too many shoulds and should-nots, have contributed to the loss of the essence of the old religions.

When you start believing in a magical world, you can simply start behaving as if the world is full of miracles, mysteries, and unknowns. A clear example is the channeling we are doing now. Jeroen, with his highly developed mental energy body, was and still is quite skeptical about spiritual affairs. When his life was at a dead end, he chose to follow a course in spiritual development.[10] He was not at all certain that what he was learning was real.

At first, what motivated him was his discovery that other people who took the course were pleasant and open, and that he felt accepted by them. Actually, his soul arranged for this to happen, which at that time, of course, he did not know. During this course, miracles started to happen in his life and he felt happier and luckier. At the same time, he discovered that he was not going crazy and that he could still function in the normal world. Perhaps he could not always tell people about all of his new knowledge, but he could still function well in his job and in his relationships with other people.

When he first started channeling, he thought he was making it all up. However, the reactions of people for whom he channeled and the evident quality of what he produced made him realize that something more than just imagination was going on. How could it be possible to get such precise information about things he could not possibly know? So remaining somewhat skeptical, he just continued on this path, and as you can see this book is one of the results.

JEROEN KUYPER

Let rationality be your friend

With this personal account, we want to clarify that you do not have to be a total believer. In fact, a bit of skepticism is not a bad thing. After all, a critical sense makes it easier to distinguish between higher information and more personality-based information. When your intuitive energy body develops more, your critical sense will become less important. However, we do not propose that you let go of all rationality. The mental energy body with its rationality is just fine. The only problem is that an overly developed mental energy body may block the development of the intuitive energy body.

A person who does not believe in the magical aspects of the world will find it nearly impossible to change his beliefs instantly. However, when the personality keeps resisting the soul's directions to follow its path, instant change can happen. In such a case, the Divine Power of the universe may intervene by creating either an accident or a miracle. Often people who experience accidents or miracles suddenly open to the magical aspects of life. Unfortunately, for many people the mental energy body is so greatly developed that they even overlook or invalidate miracles.

Some people are less skeptical and more open to miracles. Mostly, those people who had challenging childhoods have learned to be more open to reality as it really is. People who grow up in easy conditions often see only a safe, limited part of life. People who grow up in more difficult conditions learn more quickly about all aspects of life. Since they know that life does not always give what would seem reasonable or predictable they become more open-minded. Often they are less skeptical about and more open to the magical aspects of life. Froukje had a difficult childhood. Her father died early and her mother had to work. One of the positive results of this is that she has an open mind.

Jeroen and Froukje's meeting and subsequent partnership was prearranged—for reasons including the completion of this work. Froukje's persistence in asking the guides questions and taking the information seriously helps Jeroen overcome his skepticism.

Whether you have someone to help you or not, we suggest that you just start to make your world magical. You will see that there really is much magic in the world, and that new and interesting pathways can open for you. You will find that what you are doing is not strange and that you can still lead a normal life. All you are doing is opening yourself to the bigger reality just beyond your own reality. As you do this, you will be able to access more of the ancient knowledge again.

Science is developing in this direction also. For example, medical scientists are now starting to study herbs and plants that tribal healers have used for many centuries. Unfortunately, medical researchers focus only on isolating those parts of a plant which they perceive as active ingredients. They do not see that the powers of light and forces of nature are also important parts of the healing power of these plants. When you just isolate the active ingredients of a plant, you do not utilize the plant's full healing power. Moreover, tribal healers enhance the healing capacity of a plant by using it in connection with nature spirits. Unfortunately, medical scientists still ignore these important aspects of healing with plants.

Nevertheless, scientists are becoming more interested in and more accepting of spiritual phenomena. Scientists are becoming more open as a result of the new energy waves coming to earth and the development of the intuitive body.

We are now coming to the end of our book. We hope that

we helped our channels and our readers to find more ways to get in touch with Divine Energy. We sincerely hope that you continue on your path of joy and growth. For now, we wish you a very happy future. Please know that every one of you may call upon us anytime you wish, and we will help you. We assist you even if you do not ask, but your asking makes it easier for us to be more precise in our assistance. Our love is ever present for everyone and, of course, that includes you.

This is the end of the book. For now, we say good-bye to you with all our love and light.

44.
Words of Good-bye

Squaw Meadow Trail

Welcome, this is Phylos. We greet you with our message of love and support from our realms on this mountain. You can feel that the energy here is very high at this time of day. We welcome you to the mountain for your last walk during this trip, and we wish to express our gratitude for your work. Saint Germain enjoyed supporting you both, especially Froukje, during this stay.

You have translated our transmissions in a pure form, which we think many will understand. We hold a focus for our material to become an inspiring and enjoyable book that reaches the right persons and supports them on their souls' path.

Our love and our support are always with you. We welcome you back at any time to proceed with the work. We have many more things to tell you about life on earth and in other realms.

You two are a wonderful team for us. Of course, we have known that this is how things were meant to be, and we actually directed you to meet us here to help us deliver this material to the world. We want to compliment you for the dedicated way you have worked together—with Froukje holding the energy and Jeroen translating our transmissions into language.

We suggest that you find a nice place now to enjoy the sunset, and we wish you a most happy journey back home—which we, of course, will also support with our light. We hope and expect to see you back here many more times; we have much more material to teach.

For now, our dictation ends. We say good-bye to you for now with all our light and with great love for the beings that you are.

BIOGRAPHIES

Jeroen Kuyper was born in 1955 in the Netherlands. He received a master's degree in clinical psychology at the University of Groningen. He now works as a psychotherapist in an outreach department of a psychiatric clinic.

Froukje Buma was born in 1959 in the Netherlands, where she too obtained a master's degree in clinical psychology at the University of Groningen. She worked at the university for twelve years, teaching and coaching students, faculty, and family doctors.

Although both were successful in their jobs, they each experienced crises in their personal lives and were looking for more meaning and growth. In 1993, the two attended the *Awakening Your Light Body* course created by Sanaya Roman and Duane Packer and their guides Orin and DaBen.[11] This course was deeply transformational for Froukje and Jeroen and led them to discover their own channeling and healing capacities. It also brought them together as a couple.

They began to work as a team and formed a "light center" named *Israna* with which to take their spiritual work out into the world. Since 1996, they have taught channeling, the *Awakening Your Light Body* course, and its sequels. Since 1997, they have visited the United States twice a year to channel the Phylos books, and to participate in Light Body seminars in Oregon.

In 1996, Froukje left her job at the university to open a practice in psychotherapy, spiritual healing, and meditation. In her work, she channels many light beings, including the Ascended Master Saint Germain, the Goddess Isis, and Archangel Gabriel. Froukje's channelings are directed to healing and to helping people on their spiritual path.

Jeroen has reduced his regular job to part time in order to devote more time to his spiritual work. He channels a number of guides and masters, including the Ascended Masters Phylos and Kuthumi.

A few years ago, when Donald Schnell/Prema Baba Swamiji read an early draft of Earth Changes, he declared enthusiastically that it was "the definitive guidebook to help prepare readers to enter the higher vibrational frequency". Recently, he initiated Jeroen and Froukje into Babaji's Modern Order of Swamis.

ENERGY POINT

We hope you will enjoy the small blue and yellow circle on the back cover. Phylos requested that we put a point of light on each of our books. Erik Kleinepier very kindly created this point for us.

The point is a focal point for lines of light which Phylos extends to all readers, and for lines of light which all readers naturally extend to one another.

When you look at this point, feel your connection with the masters, with everyone else reading the book, and with all light workers on the planet and beyond. Imagine that you and all these beings form a web of lines of light. You may radiate your light into this web. When you do this, you reinforce the growing network of light connections on the planet and receive light back for your own growth.

JEROEN KUYPER

CONTACT US

We invite you to visit our website.
www.ascendedmasters.nl

Order CDs of Phylos's and St. Germain's guided meditations.
Learn about our courses and seminars (with Jeroen & Froukje and the ascended masters).
Read about our upcoming books.
Get the latest news and information about the masters' teachings.

We would love to hear from you! We would be most grateful to receive your feedback on *Earth Changes*. And, since we live in the Netherlands, where North American book reviews are difficult to access, we would very much appreciate receiving copies of any reviews you might come across.

In love and Light,
Jeroen and Froukje

Email   info@ascendedmasters.nl

Fax (within the Netherlands)   0-592 612153
Fax (from other countries)   +31-592 612153
                                (Note: Replace the plus sign
                                with the access code for

international calls from your
location.)

Mailing address	Jeroen Kuyper and Froukje Buma Hugo de Vriesweg 45 9751 PR Haren (Gn) Netherlands

NOTES

[1] The seminar, which Jeroen and Froukje attended in Ashland, was one of a series called Awakening Your Light Body developed by Dr. Duane Packer and Sanaya Roman with their guides, DaBen and Orin. Many students of this work have wonderful spiritual experiences. For more information, see www.orindaben.com, or contact LuminEssence Creations, P.O. Box 1310, Medford, OR 97501, Telephone (541) 770-6700.

[2] According to some books, the ascended masters' Radiant Temple is located in Mount Shasta, and the entrance to that temple is on a slope somewhere on the mountain. E.g. Van Valer, Nola: *My meetings with the Masters on Mount Shasta.* Seekers & Servers, 1994.

[3] Editor's note: Since time and space do not exist in the dimensions on which Phylos exists, he can address both Jeroen and Froukje, the channels through whom he speaks, and the "future" readers of the book simultaneously. Conventional English verb tenses cannot describe this phenomenon.

[4] We had purchased the booklet *Sacred Spots of Mount Shasta* (publisher unknown), which contained stories about this area and other areas that we visited. Froukje had not yet read the booklet.

[5] Phylos regards time as the fourth dimension.

[6] Phylos speaks of the physical, etheric, emotional, mental, and intuitive energy bodies. These are the energy fields which constitute your human vehicle on earth.

[7] Seth is an out-of-body teacher. Seth and his channel, Jane Roberts, created a series of books including *The Nature of Personal Reality*, Amber-Allen, 1994.

[8] A fractal is a geometric pattern that is repeated in ever smaller versions of itself to produce irregular shapes and surfaces that cannot be created using classical geometry. Fractals are primarily used to create computer models of irregular patterns and structures in nature.

[9] In 1930, Saint Germain appeared to writer Guy Ballard near this spring. In his book *Unveiled Mysteries,* Saint Germain Press, he described his encounter with Saint Germain. Ballard's pen name was Godfre Ray King.

[10] The "course in spiritual development" referred to here is the Awakening Your Light Body course, developed by Duane Packer and Sanaya Roman with their guides, DaBen and Orin. See note #1.

[11] For more information, see note #1.

Made in the USA